Exploring #Connectedness: Millennials and Generation Z

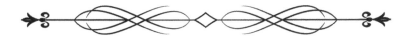

Darina Callanan
and
Susan McKenna

With Guest Chapters from
Dr. Phil Noone
Catherine Fitzgibbon
Jennifer Murphy
Meghann Scully

Edited by
Dr. Niall MacGiolla Bhuí

All rights reserved.
Published by TheDocCheck.Com
For further information re national & international distribution:
Susan at www.thedoccheck.com
Follow us on Twitter: @ThesisClinic Instagram @DissertationDoctor

Printed in the Republic of Ireland using sustainable forestry materials.
First Edition 2021
ISBN 978-1-8383142-7-9

Edited by Niall MacGiolla Bhuí, PhD
Cover Design by Niall MacGiolla Bhuí
Cover Photogragh by Eddie Kavanagh

*TheDocCheck.Com is committed to inclusion and diversity.
* We use only papers that are natural, renewable and recyclable products
and made from wood grown in sustainable forests. We ask of our Print
partners that they ensure the logging and manufacturing processes conform
to the environmental regulations of the country of origin.

About This Book Series

Our aspiration is that this #Connectedness Series will facilitate readers, and particularly students of third level Human Resources courses, to understand the complexity of the generations that are Gen Z and Millennials.

Karl Mannheim published "Das Problem der Generationen" in 1923 (translated to English in 1952) and noted a generation was defined as a group of people that had collectively experienced a "tempo of change" at a young age. This tends to derive from very significant historical events that, in some ways, altered the very status quo concerning external environments or method of 'doing' things (Mannheim, 1952).

The current generations of the past nine decades or so include some exciting titles; the Silent Generation (people in their-upper 70s through early-90s), the Boomers (people in their upper-50s through mid-70s), Generation X (people in their early-40s through mid-50s), the Millennials or Generation Y (people in their mid-20s to upper-30s), and Generation Z (people aged about 8 to 23) (Dimock, 2019).

I was born into Generation X (those of us born between 1965-1980) and, along with my peers, have witnessed many globally notable events, including examples such as the

i

momentous fall of the Berlin Wall and communism. I remember clearly the beginnings of the HIV/AIDS epidemic when I was a university student. Such phenomena have greatly influenced my thinking around the power of the individual and collective thought and action. Connections and connecting.

I bought my first house (as a home, not as an investment property) in my mid-twenties. I was fortunate to secure tenured employment in my mid-twenties. At the time, these were considered not only to be hugely influential in life but somehow the natural order of things. But is this the case now? Can it be the case? Will it *ever* be the case again for youthful workers?

Millennials (those born between 1981-1994) have also experienced and been directly affected by seismic events such as the global recession of 2007-2009 and now again with another global occurrence; COVID-19. They have been very significantly and I believe disproportionately affected by the massive layoffs and furloughs, as have their younger peers.

Generation Z is referred to as the iGeneration, iGenners, GenZ, and Generation Now and consists of those born in the mid-1990s through the late 2010s. This is the college/university-aged generation (Seemiller & Grace, 2016) who grew up with access to more and more complex and disruptive technology (Looper, 2011). Ironically, this generation is the safest (in the western world) compared to previous generations when one considers a range of health and safety statistics, but are more likely to be anxious and depressed and to die through suicide due to their 'emotional fragility' as identified by Twenge (2017). This is both perplexing and deeply shocking.

This series is designed to be valid for 1) the individual looking to enhance knowledge about Millennials and Gen Z and 2) the interested Human Resources student and professional who do not want to read purely theoretical material but are interested in acquiring valuable references to scholarly material. Make no mistake; lives are complex for Millennials and Gen Z (Eisenberger, Lieberman & Williams, 2003). The age of the Internet and 'wearable technologies' presents very many challenges. In all of this, Millennials and Gen Z are trying to make sense of themselves and their place in the world.

It's been a pleasure editing the diverse chapters from my colleagues. Therefore, the series itself is intended not just to be 'books to read' but also as reference guides. We do not demand you read this book in a narrative arc; feel free to dip in and out of whatever chapter takes your fancy. We're not precious about individual chapter ownership, and each chapter can be read individually and out of order without losing the integrity of the book's theme of connectedness. Enjoy.

- Dr. Niall MacGiolla Bhuí, Editor.

References and Suggested Reading

Dimock, M. (2019, January 17). Defining generations: Where Millennials end and Generation Z begins. Retrieved May 15th, 2021, from https://www.pewresearch.org/fact- tank/2019/01/17/where-millennials-end-and-generation-z-begins/

Eisenberger, N. I., Lieberman, M. D., & Williams, K. D. (2003). Does rejection hurt? An fMRI study of social exclusion. Science, 302, 290–292. https://doi.org/10.1126/science.1089134

Harris, K. "A New Generation of Workers: Preparing for Generation Z in the Workplace" (2020). Senior Theses. 335. https://scholarcommons.sc.edu/senior_theses/335

Looper, L. (2011). How Generation Z Works. How Stuff Works. Retrieved from https://people.howstuffworks.com/culture-traditions/generation-gaps/generation-z.htm Accessed April 12th 2021.

Mannheim, K. (1952). The problem of generations. In P. Kecskemeti (Vol. Ed.), *Essays on the sociology of knowledge: Collected works: ume 5,* (pp. 276-322). New York: Routledge.

Miller, J. (2018, November). 10 Things You Need to Know About Gen Z. *HR Magazine.*

Seemiller, C., & Grace, M. (2016). Generation Z goes to college. San Francisco: Jossey-Bass.

Twenge, J. M. (2017). iGen : Why today's super-connected kids are growing up less rebellious, more tolerant, less happy and completely unprepared for adulthood and what that means for the rest of us. New York, NY, US: Atria Books.

Williams, A. (2015). Move over, Millennials, here comes Generation Z. Sept 18, (New York Times), 1–7. Retrieved from http://www.nytimes.com/2015/09/20/fashion/move-over- millennials-here-comes-generation-z.html?_r=0 Accessed April 10th 2021.

Zapier Editorial Team. (2020). *Misunderstood generations: what Millennials and Gen Z actually think about work.* Zapier. Retrieved from https://zapier.com/blog/digital-natives-r

Table of Contents

Exploring #Connectedness:
Millennials and Generation Z

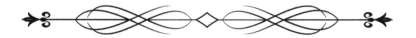

Darina Callanan, MA.,
and Susan McKenna, B.A. Dip. SocSci

"The young have become the pigeons of the public realm, only remarked upon for their poor mental health or when they leave litter in a park."

— The Guardian 6.4.2021 Zoe Williams

Introduction

This is the first in our series of volumes from our consulting staff and friends of our DocCheck.Com service based in Galway and Limerick, Ireland, on the theme of #connectedness. In this, we look to Millennials and Generation Z and explore themes pertinent to these specific cohorts. We recognise that global society is, to use a postmodern term, 'embedded' in a technologically vast and volatile environment where the employability of workers is constructed on their levels of adaptability (Savickas, 2011). This has resulted in an increasingly fragmented world that, unfortunately, advocates separateness from the human condition where the virtual world is becoming the 'go to' existence.

We suggest an increasing and widespread sense of hopelessness with fragmentation of both the outer and inner worlds of Millennials and Gen Z, particularly regarding identity. On a positive note, there is a growing curiosity to locate meaning and connectedness.

With change comes possibility. Workplaces are dramatically changing as the global COVID-19 pandemic has altered everything for us, and we are all trying to make sense of this new terrain. While most organisations will enjoy the benefits of a multi-generational workforce, it is noteworthy to mention the requirement for regular feedback is particularly significant about managing a Millennial and Gen Z workforce whereby the need for validation and positive reinforcement has been driven by the impact of social media in their lives when compared to employees of other generations.

In this, there are winners and losers. Pre pandemic, we had witnessed the phenomenon of the rise of 'influencers' (Scully,

2021). We had seen an increasing interest in the environment and sustainability, in the ethical sourcing of food and the use of social media by Millennials and Generation Zers. Are these still core concerns just one year on from the first recorded cases of COVID-19?

At the time of completion of this first book in our series, it is evident that pandemic-related work shutdowns have disproportionately affected both Millennials and Gen Z, especially younger members. The recently published Deloitte Global Millennial Survey (2020) notes that 'almost 30% of Gen Zs and a quarter of younger millennials (25–30 years old) who took our pulse survey in late April or early May reported either losing their jobs or having been placed on temporary, unpaid leave. At that point, about one in five millennials around the world had been put out of work." (Deloitte, 2021: 1).

Millennials

You're going to frequently come across the word 'Millennial' in this book, and it's a term that remains a little vague despite its pervasive use in the media. The word Millennial has gained currency in the past few years and refers to a generation that is broadly characterised by increased use and familiarity with three things; communications, media and, in particular, digital technologies. The term was coined some thirty years ago by Neil Howe and William Strauss. Depending on whose research you read, you'll find the term denoting those born in the 1970s, 1980s and even into the 1990s. The U.S. Census Bureau defines Millennials as people born between 1982 and 2000, and the statistics are staggering. The research has two categories; younger Millennials aged 18 to 24 and older Millennials aged 25 to 36.

Up to 50% of Millennials living in the United States now consider themselves 'content creators', and 75% share content online. Their lives are lived out online. Seventy-eight per cent of Millennials would choose to spend money on a 'desirable experience' over buying something that is 'desirable'. So, the message from the research is clear; Millennials love three things; creating, sharing, and capturing memories. Indeed, if we were to attempt to sum up, in a few words, the very diverse backgrounds shared by Millennials, it might well be in the phrase, 'What's the WIFI code?' (MacGiolla Bhuí, 2018).

Millennials like to have access to communications. Smartphones and Tablets are now considered an essential and integrative part of their user's daily routines, becoming a primary conduit for connecting with friends, family, gathering information, purchasing and gaming.

Mass communication is now an everyday reality, and

Ireland has the highest rate of smartphone usage per capita in Western Europe. Facebook, Linked In, and Instagram, to name but three platforms, are at our fingertips, and we can upload and share photos, data and files in real-time. You'll either love this or find it incredibly annoying.

Change is so quick, so deep, and so profound that one cannot blame teens and young adults for being confused. Everyone in this space needs to become informed - as informed as Millennials and Gen Z if this is possible. It seems to us that a large part of trying to understand Millenial and Gen Z mental health lies in both cohorts living so much of their lives through the filtered lens of virtual reality where every image is carefully curated and morphed until the very best image possible is sent hurtling out through cyberspace.

Millennials and Gen Z trust recommendations more from friends than any other source and regularly go online to confirm this. They enjoy digital coupon life in a way that is alien to those just a generation behind them. User-generated content on websites profoundly influences Millennials and Gen Z – as distinct from owners and supposed 'experts' or celebrity endorsements. And, why not when the average person now checks his or her smartphone 43 times daily. We need to get to know, intimately, the behavioural patterns of Millenials and Gen Z if we want to reach out to them and engage them successfully.

Gen Z

'Generation Z' (known hereafter as Gen Z) is the working cohort that is identified as those born after 1995 (Chillakuri and Mahanandia, 2018), comprising some 32% of the global population. Gen Z has come to the attention of multiple stakeholders, entrepreneurs, colleges, business leaders, and human resource practitioners as it is such an influential group (Chillakuri, 2020b). How interesting that Gen Z is named after the last letter in the alphabet. This generation 'marks the end of clearly defined roles, traditions and experiences' (Sladek and Grabinger, 2014).

Current research that has sought to define the specific characteristics of Gen Z remains embryonic (Dwivedula et al., 2016), with contention around concepts and constructs in terms of understanding of the segment's attitudes, preferences and behaviours (Chillakuri, 2020).

Gen Z is the first fully digital generation, and with over 61 million Gen Zs coming into the workplace, you better be sure things are about to change (Cummings, 2016). According to a recent survey carried out by Deloitte, employers will need to have a new mindset when it comes to Gen Z (Gomez et al., 2019). The upcoming generations will not be interested in the traditional workplace practices of office-bound 9 am to 5 pm. That much is sure.

With Gen Z coming into the workplace, employers need to familiarise themselves with what Gen Zs want and expect from the workplace (Bassiouni and Hackley, 2014). A characteristic continually associated with Gen Z is being connected through high-tech technology - and communicating over existing social media platforms (Adecco, 2015). It is essential for employers to change the way of 'sending emails and make the communication in the workplace more personal for the new Gen Z employees. Many people might assume that Gen Z is somewhat lazy. Still, interestingly, in a recent survey with 400 Gen Z college students, 80% of the students stated that they would still work even if they had enough money to live comfortably (Coogan and Crowley-Henry, 2020).

The real question here is, do we know what this Gen Z will bring to the workforce? There is very little known about the current generation's attitudes, characteristics, needs and working style. Gen Z will be a strong workforce, and there may be implications with Millennials and Gen Z with their different views and behaviours about the workplace (Jiří, 2020). Sladek and Grabinger (2014) expressed the critical difference between Millennials and Gen Z; thus, "Gen Y is full of dreamers; Gen Z is full of realists". The idea that success is about trying to complete a task rather than meeting it creates a sense of artificial entitlement. No wonder Millennials are questioning their reality and trying to reshape it in a way that makes sense from within their somewhat limited context (Housel, 2017).

Dr Jean Twenge, a Professor of Psychology at San Diego University, wrote about *Generation Me* in 2006 and explored what is understood to be Millenial culture when she located a notable cultural shift in the mid-1970s public-school curriculum in the United States. Thus, the oldest Millennials were aged between 39 and 40 years old in 2017. The last year of the "Baby Boomers," also known as the "me generation," is officially 1963. Anyone born after 1964 through the mid-70s is called "Generation X" (Housel, 2017).

Writing in Mental Health for Millennials in 2017, US-based scholar, Rebecca Housel, observes that post-modernism acknowledges the importance of every individual through their positionality. But, let's conclude on a welcome finding from the Deloitte 2020 Survey, which found "Despite the individual challenges and personal sources of anxiety that millennials and Gen Zs are facing, they have remained focused on larger societal issues, both before and after the onset of the pandemic" (Deloitte, 2020: 9).

References and Suggested Reading

Adecco (2015). Generation Z vs. Millennials. USA: Adecco.

Bassiouni, DH, Hackley, C (2014). "Generation Z" children's adaptation to digital consumer culture: a critical literature review. Journal of Customer Behaviour 13(2): 113–33.

Bencsik, A., Horvath -Csikos, G. & Timea, J., (2016). Y and Z Generations at Workplaces. *Journal of Competitiveness*, 8(3), pp. 90-106.

Bernier, L., (2015). Getting ready for gen Z. *Canadian HR Reporter* , 16 November , p. 1.

Cates, S. V., (2014). The young and the restless: Why don't Millennials join unions. *International Journal of Business and Public Administration* , 11(2), pp. 107-119.

Chillakuri, B. and Mahanandia, R. (2018). Generation Z entering the workforce: the need for sustainable strategies in maximizing their talent. *Human Resource Management International Digest*, 26(4), pp.34-38.

Chillakuri, Bharat. (2020). Understanding Generation Z expectations for effective onboarding. Journal of Organizational Change Management. ahead-of-print. 10.1108/JOCM-02-2020-0058.

Chillakuri, Bharat. (2020b). Examining the Role of Supervisor Support on Generation Z's Intention to Quit. American Business Review. 23. 408-430.10.37625/abr.23.2.408-430.

Cummings, C (2016). Video killed the TV star: Gen Z turns away from traditional TV and embraces digital. ADWEEK 57(9): 11.

Deloitte, (2021). The Deloitte Global Millennial Survey 2020. Resilient generations hold the key to creating a better normal. Deloitte.

Dwivedula, Ravikiran & Bredillet, Christophe & Müller, Ralf. (2016). Personality and work motivation as determinants of project success: the mediating role of organisational and professional commitment. International Journal of Management Development. 1. 229. 10.1504/IJMD.2016.076553.

Housel, R. (2017). Let's talk about sex baby: Millennials and sexuality in the US. Mental Health for Millennials, 56-69, Vol 1. Galway: Book Hub Publishing.

Iorgulescu, M.-C., (2016). Generation Z and its perception of work. *Cross-Cultural Management Journal*, 18(1), pp. 47-54.

Kutlák, Jiří. (2020). Motivation Drivers and Barriers of Generation Z at Work: Mebs Method. 322-331. 10.7441/dokbat.2020.27.

Manpower Group, (2016). Millenial Careers:2020 Vision Facts, Figures and Practical Advice from Workforce Experts , s.l.: Manpower Group.

MacGiolla Bhuí, N. (2018). The Search for self-identity and flow in the millennial space: Filtered incrementalism. Mental Health for Millennials, 14-22, Vol 2. Galway: Book Hub Publishing.

Merriman , M., (2015). Gen Z: The Next Big Disruptor. *WWD*, 210(6), p. 86.

Mitchell, K., (2016). We Are All Gen Z--- and Y and X. *HR Magazine* , 61(10), pp. 18-19.

RTE, 10.1.2020. https://www.rte.ie/brainstorm/2019/1003/1080884-meet-your-new-workmates-generation-zs-views-on-work-and-careers/ Reporting on a study by Coogan and Crowley- Henry. Accessed April 2nd 2021.

Savickas, Mark. (2011). Constructing careers: Actor, agent, and author. Journal of Employment Counseling. 48. 10.1002/j.2161-1920.2011.tb01109.x.

Scully, M. (2021). This volume.

Singh , P., Rai, S. & Bhandarker, A., (2012). Millennials and the Workplace: Challenges for Architecting the Organisations of Tomorrow. 1st ed. New Delhi: Sage Publications.

Sladek, S and Grabinger, A. (2014) Gen Z. The First Generation of the 21st Century Has Arrived. https://www.xyzuniversity.com/wp-content/uploads/2018/08/GenZ_Final-dl1.pdf

Stuckey, C., (2016). Preparing Leaders for Gen Z. *Training Journal* , pp.

33-35.

Suleman , R. & Nelson, B., 2011. Motivation the Millennials: Tapping into the potential of the youngest generation. *Leader to Leader,* 2011(62), pp. 39-44.

Thompson, C. & Brodie Gregory , J., (2012). Managing Millennials: A Framework for Improving Attraction, Motivation and Retention. *The Psychologist-Manager Journal ,* 15(4), pp. 237-246.

Tulgan , B., (2013). *Meet Generation Z: the second generation within the giant "Millenial" cohort.* Retrieved at http://rainmakerthinking.com/assets/uploads/2013/10/Gen-Z-Whitepaper.pdf ed. s.l.:Rainmaker Thinking.

Twenge, J. M. (2006). Generation Me: Why today's young Americans are more confident, assertive, entitled--and more miserable than ever before. New York, NY: Free Press.

Tysjac , K., (2017). Get ready for Gen Z. *Journal of Accountancy ,* 224(2), pp. 1-2.

Are Millennials and Generation Z Satisfied and Motivated by the same things in the Workplace? An Exploratory Commentary

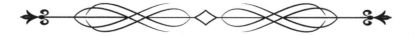

Darian Callanan, MA.

Introduction

When we think of the workplace and Millennials and Gen Z, one question comes to mind; are they motivated and satisfied by the same workplace? It is evident from the research and my practice in HR that both generations have significant differences across several core areas. Still, can HR 'fill two needs with the one deed' when it comes to motivating and providing job satisfaction to the two generations in the workplace? Let's look at the meaning of rewards in the workplace, motivation, job satisfaction, and probe to see if there are fundamental differences between the two generations.

Total Reward and Reward Management Systems

The theoretical basis of total rewards originates from a holistic approach that captures both financial and non-financial rewards that a company may provide to employees (Tsede and Kutin, 2013). It is necessary to look at total reward strategies, as it is a combination of both intrinsic and extrinsic motivation that organisations use to attract, motivate and, ultimately, retain employees (WorldatWork, 2015). Rumpel and Medcof (2006) state that total rewards aim to embrace everything employees' value from their work. Mabaso and Dlamini, (2018) suggest that total rewards assist in the organisational commitment of employees and Omotayo, et al. (2014) further add that organisational commitment is an essential element as it effectively results in higher employee commitment, increased retention and increasing job satisfaction, which in turn improves performance. A total reward strategy is a focused plan which distributes resources and tailors' activities with the specific aim of achieving a high-level performance amongst employees.

Reward management systems (RMS) can be considered one of the primary methods of attaining control as it impacts the existing behaviours and attitudes of employees and organisational culture. Taylor (2015) observes that a reward represents a tangible benefit that identifies effort, service or achievement. Halilbegovic et al. (2018) note that companies endeavour to convince their employees to perform effectively by offering rewards for agreeable performance and, in turn, rebuffing employees for unacceptable work.

Rewards can range from the obvious monetary incentives such as bonuses to non-monetary rewards such as flexible working hours (Bartol and Srivastava, 2002). According to Shafiq and Naseem (2011), reward systems should be aligned with an employee's perceived favourable outcome if its purpose is to motivate employees to maximise their potential in their role. Armstrong (2007) suggested that reward practice will enhance commitment, motivation, improve employee behaviour and increase job engagement. More recently, De Waal and Jansen (2013) argue that the proponents of bonuses and the importance of monetary rewards increases productivity and performance within an organisation. In an article published in the American Management Association (2014), it is suggested that organisations must reenergise compensation and benefits that are being offered to satisfy the needs and wants of each generation's unique attitudes, values and perspectives concerning work.

This research involved the use of semi-structured, one-to-one interviews of a sample of this cohort of the labour market, specifically a group of Gen Z and Millennial employees. To select the participants for the research study, emails were sent to 24 individuals, twelve Millennials and twelve Gen Z. Furthermore, an explanation was given about reward management systems and the two-generational cohorts. Seven individuals replied and agreed to take part in the interview process. The participants chosen were aged between 21- 36 years old. A set of fifteen questions were explored with the participants via face-to-face interviews. The participants interviewed work across various sectors such as Technology, Healthcare, Human Resources and Recruitment.

The objective of which was to gain an understanding of their perception of the reward structures available within their workplace. The Gen Z participants believe that Millennials value money over other forms of rewards. The above statements are also at variance with Schroth (2019), who argues that Millennials tend to place very significant value on work-life balance. The Millennial participants have expressed the belief that Gen Z tends to desire superior tangible rewards - and that management will find it difficult to accommodate those desires as they expect Gen Z will demand more reward benefits than the company is offering, resulting in the generational cohort potentially leaving an organisation.

Alzyoud (2018) suggests that RMS are implemented within organisations to increase motivation and job satisfaction amongst employees. However, this is adjacent to the opinion of Millennial participants, as they proclaimed that they do not find RMS motivating. On the other hand, the Gen Z participants agree with the statement by Alzyoud (2018) and find that reward management systems are effectively encouraging, motivating them to work more efficiently. Conversely, Schroth (2019) argues that Gen Z have a somewhat romantic picture of the workplace regarding their needs potentially being met - and management will face very significant challenges with regards to satisfying these needs and wants. According to Doyle (2021), Gen Z wants things such as clear career progression paths, upskilling opportunities and most importantly, a company culture that focuses on the wellbeing of their employees. It is clear that both generations have different wants and needs when it comes to rewards and this is very likely going to challenge the status quo.

Motivation

When it comes to motivating employees in the workplace, it can always be a challenge for supervisors and management. Is it possible to satisfy everyone in the workplace when it comes to employee engagement initiatives? The answer is probably no. As the workplace comprises a mixture of generations, a "one size fits all" approach is likely to prove insufficient due to different cohort preferences. It is crucial for us to understand what these differences are and ask the question, is it possible to get that perfect balance when it comes to motivating the ever-changing and dynamic workforce?

According to Jones and George (2011) motivation comprises psychological forces that determine an individual's behaviour, effort and levels of persistence within an organisation. In today's (post)modern workforce, motivation is the key to achieving competitive advantage, increasing productivity and, ultimately, increasing organisation profits. For motivation to be maximised, employees must be fully engaged and, in a sense, buy into the work culture.

Intrinsic and Extrinsic Motivation

When looking at how both generations are motivated in the workplace, it is essential to look at the two main types of motivation: intrinsic and extrinsic. Locke and Schattke, (2018) suggest that intrinsic motivation means wanting or liking activity for its own sake, separate from any precise outcome level.

Barile, et al. (2018) add that intrinsic motivation occurs when individuals believe that they will originate intrinsic value from the action. Although intrinsically motivated activities are goal-focused, the fulfilment and pursuit of the goal are no longer separate; and the individual acknowledges the pursuing of the activity as essentially attaining the goal (Woolley and Fishbach, 2018).

There are several theories that prompt debate about intrinsic motivation. However, the most significant and widely known theory include Deci and Ryan's (1985, 2000) Self-Determination Theory (SDT). The SDT theory draws attention to the evaluation of an individual's actions. The SDT theory suggests that intrinsic motivation levels are higher when there is better task engagement and a greater focus on goals. The SDT recognises that the explicit means of expressing and satisfying basic needs vary considerably through a prevailing culture and context. Also, the SDT proposes to help understand how social and cultural factors facilitate an individual's sense of determination and initiative. Lloyd et al. (2017) suggest that intrinsic motivation is linked with greater training outcomes. Dysvik and Kuvaas (2008) add that employees with higher levels of intrinsic motivation have an optimistic relationship with apparent training prospects.

Antonioli, et al., (2016) state that extrinsic motivation refers to factors that affect individual behaviour and incentives produced by the need to attain an outcome. Extrinsic motivation can be defined as that process where individuals will live up to their needs in return for physical rewards - which are provided by organisations; such as salary, bonuses, supplementary benefits, e.g. a company car, and development opportunities (Priya and Eshwar, 2014). Moreover, (Mickel and Barron, 2008) argue some of the early studies in motivation proposed that extrinsic motivation was a more powerful way of controlling employee behaviour and also more effective in motivating employees than intrinsic motivation.

To achieve optimum motivation within the workplace, organisations need to consider a permanent mixture of intrinsic and extrinsic motivation, influencing an individual's level of job satisfaction (Wong et al., 1998). The most important factor in any organisation is the workforce - therefore, it is essential for the organisation to ensure that employees are motivated, whether through intrinsic or extrinsic factors. - and this achievement facilitates the receipt of an intrinsic and/ or extrinsic outcome.

Many organisations have noticed that the Gen Zs have different motivating factors than their Millennial co-workers. With the power of social media and technology at their fingertips, they can see what their Gen Z peers are receiving elsewhere, resulting in them not settling for less. If organisations are not offering Gen Z employees meaningful career opportunities and fail to deliver the needs such as work flexibility they desire, Gen Z will not hesitate to leave and seek employment elsewhere (Pelta, 2019).

Job Satisfaction

Most organisations in Ireland are currently managing a multigenerational workforce and with that comes generational clashes. Job satisfaction is vital to any organisation because if you have a happy workforce, the research shows that there will be an increase in solid performances and outputs. By 2025, Millennials will make up 75 per cent of the workforce, and we will see an increased exit of both the Baby Boomers and Generation X employees (Anugrah et al., 2020). Firstly, organisations need to understand what job satisfaction means for their workforce and plan accordingly. Job satisfaction is one of the most extensively researched aspects of organisational behaviour because of the critical role in employment (Fogliasso, et al., 2013). Locke (1976) defines job satisfaction as an individual's positive emotional state and attitude, which is achieved through the accomplishments of work experience and performing tasks successfully. On the other hand, job dissatisfaction ascends when these expectations are not met (Kreitner and Kinicki, 2003).

Sawitri et al., (2016) propose that levels of job satisfaction depend on an individual's variable levels of satisfaction. Accordingly, if an individual desires something, they will be motivated to take action in order to achieve those expectations. In comparison, Applebaum, et al., (2010) argue that physical environmental factors such as noise, temperature, humidity etc. and work-related stress invariably impact on job satisfaction levels and, in turn, could potentially prompt turnover. Kurniawaty et al., (2019) further state that there is evidence that supports that the physical environment does indeed affect the job satisfaction levels - but may also affect employee performance, behaviour and psychological stress.

Factors that Influence Job Satisfaction

As discussed extensively throughout this study, job satisfaction is one of the critical components in achieving engagement, commitment and retention, often resulting in a broader sense of fulfilment through connectedness with the organisation. Karin Andreassi, et al., (2014) state that increasing salaries, rewards and desirable colleague performance can increase job satisfaction levels for employees. Furthermore, Singhapakdi, et al., (2015) adds that operative supervision and allocation of meaningful tasks also increase job satisfaction. Autonomy in the workplace can also influence job satisfaction.

Work autonomy can be defined as the freedom employees have when it comes to work activities and decision making in the workplace (Sia and Appu, 2015). Independence can lead to greater engagement and happiness, and management need to allow employees to think and act more independently in the workplace.

As mentioned earlier in this chapter, interviews were conducted with the Millennial and Gen Z participants to determine what they believe might constitute good strategies that an HR Department could implement to increase their job satisfaction in the workplace. The three core HR strategies and opportunities identified were; social media, feedback surveys and the creation of a diverse workplace. One of the Millennial participants observed that 'Social media is definitely a great way to attract generation Z'. Further to this, one of the Gen Z participants agreed and stated 'Social media has to be one. For example, large organisations always run campaigns on Instagram and include swipe up links which makes it easy to apply for jobs. Concerning creating a diverse workplace, another Millennial participant suggested, 'It is a great opportunity to build a unique workforce because it increases creativity and introduces a wider range of skills. A Gen Z participant relayed, 'Having a diverse workforce creates positivity in the workplace, and it is interesting working with people from different cultural backgrounds. The final opportunity presented by Human Resource management were practical surveys. A Millennial participant voiced 'HR need to utilise surveys to get feedback from the employees. I think it would benefit HR departments because they can get suggestions from the current staff'. A Gen Z participant reported, 'utilising surveys allow feedback from employees on what HR can do to improve their working environment in return for staff retention and creating a happier workplace for everybody to ease the load off coming to work'. It is apparent that there are various steps implemented by HR management to maintain a positive rapport in the workplace and, in turn, increase job satisfaction. Therefore, it is necessary to look more closely at the impact of intrinsic and extrinsic motivation in the context of job satisfaction for Millennials and Gen Z.

Millennials and Generation Z – What are the Differences?

It is worth considering that momentous historical events, which may have defined generations, can vary relative to experience and location. Costanza et al. (2012) argue that experiences of historical and cultural significance in the United States will differ from the experiences occurring in China, Russia or Brazil, which essentially raises concerns about the generalizability of generations across various cultures. Therefore, it is essential to note that different life events which occur during that generational period, and experiences, will create the goals and aspirations of that generational cohort and ultimately shape their qualities.

All generational cohorts invariably share a comparable outlook and, as the generations mature, build up a certain uniqueness that distinguishes them from previous generations. Yadav and Rai (2017) argue that differences between generations include; behavioural attributes, attitudes, work ethic, the capability of learning and motivational skills. Bencsik et al., (2016) add that Gen Z is very different to their predecessors and argues that this generation is not afraid of continuous change, as they grew up in the world of the Internet. As a result, they can intuitively process more information than Millennials. The reason why it is going to be challenging for organisations to manage the new generational cohort is due to the way that Gen Zs have grown up. They are the first generation to grow up with the Internet immediately available to them. They have access to a broader amount of knowledge than any previous generations regarding workplace practices. Benson and Brown (2011) add that these differences amongst the Millennials and Gen Z will create several complex challenges for management in effectively engaging the workforce. This relates to Busch et al. (2008), who states that there will also be issues finding a way to motivate the two-generational cohorts as Gen Z may not be encouraged in the same way as the Millennials before them. HR practices should promote the principles of participation, collaboration and inclusiveness to reach mutual growth for both the individuals and organisation.

But the main question is; can the two generations work together? When I interviewed the group of Millennials and Gen Z, they firmly believe that it is going to a challenge for both generations can operate closely together in the workplace. But why would they think organisations would face such a big challenge? Different work habits come with different generational cohorts. Millennials enjoy working as a part of a team and often use the phrase 'Two heads are better than one; however, their Gen Z peers are more in favour of a solo approach and focus on getting the work done by myself and not rely on their colleagues (Whitteberry, 2019). Therefore, with the different styles in working, we are bound to see some tension between the Millennial and Generation Z employees. A Millennial participant expressed, 'There is going to be a massive clash in the workplace, and it is going to be very challenging for managers and HR, in particular, to try manage'. The participant further added 'I feel as though they think they have similar traits to us, but they are completely different. They are self-centred and obsessed with social media. Is this overly harsh? A Gen Z participant added 'Even with the small amount of us in the workforce; you can already see a tension between the two generations. Millennials can be standoffish with Generation Z'. It is apparent from the findings that tensions exist between both generational cohorts. Although both Millennials and Gen Z believe that there will be challenges, the participants interviewed expressed the belief that if both generations work together, they could, somehow, create the ultimate functioning workplace.

It was interesting to observe how the two generational groups in my micro study perceive each other within the topics discussed. In addition, discovering which existing reward management systems fulfil the needs of both Millennial and Generation Z employees - as well as motivating them to excel in the workplace. The Millennial and Generation Z participants portrayed a somewhat pessimistic view of and towards each other. The research study highlighted the strained relationship presently existing between Millennial and Generation Z co-workers. It is evident from my exploratory empirical research that management and supervisors must discover a better way to unite the two-generational cohorts in the workplace to work effectively with each other.

One thing is for sure, and both generational cohorts need to find a way to work together. When it comes to how to motivate and provide job satisfaction to both Gen Z and Millennials, well, that is something that we still need to figure out!

References and Suggested Reading

Abraham, S. (2012). Job Satisfaction as an Antecedent to Employee Engagement. *SIES Journal of Management*, 8(2), pp.27–36.

Alzyoud, A. (2018). The Influence of Human Resource Management Practices on Employee Work Engagement. *Foundations of Management*, 10(1), pp.251-256.

American Management Association (2014), 'Leading the Four Generations at Work' *Articles and White Papers*, 11 June. [online] Available: http://www.amanet.org/training/articles/Leading-the-Four-Generations-at-Work.aspx.

Antonioli, D., Nicolli, F., Ramaciotti, L. and Rizzo, U. (2016). The Effect of Intrinsic and Extrinsic Motivations on Academics' Entrepreneurial Intention. *Administrative Sciences*, 6(4), p.15.

Anugrah Putri, A., Dhewanto, W. and Fadhil Nurdayat, I., (2020). Understanding the Role of Job Satisfaction in Workplace from Millennial Generation's Perspective toward Organizational Performance. *KnE Social Sciences.*

Applebaum, D., Fowler, S., Fiedler, N., Osinubi, O. and Robson, M. (2010). The Impact of Environmental Factors on Nursing Stress, Job Satisfaction, and Turnover Intention. *JONA: The Journal of Nursing Administration*, 40(7/8), pp.323-328.

Armstrong, M. (2007). A handbook of employee reward management and practice. London: Kogan Page.

Barile, L., Cullis, J. and Jones, P. (2018). Time Preference for Investment in the Environment: The Impact of Intrinsic Motivation. *Economic Issues*, 23(2), pp. 31–56.

Bartol, K. and Srivastava, A. (2002). Encouraging Knowledge Sharing: The Role of Organizational Reward Systems. *Journal of Leadership & Organizational Studies*, 9(1), pp. 64-76.

Bencsik, A., Juhász, T., & Horváth-Csikós, G. (2016). Y and Z

Generations at Workplaces. *Journal of Cryptology, 6,* 90-106.

Benson, J. and Brown, M. (2011). Generations at work: are there differences and do they matter?. *The International Journal of Human Resource Management,* 22(9), pp.1843-1865.

Busch, P., Venkitachalam, K. and Richards, D. (2008). Generational differences in soft knowledge situations: status, need for recognition, workplace commitment and idealism. *Knowledge and Process Management,* 15(1), pp.45-58.

Costanza, D. P., Badger, J. M., Fraser, R. L., Severt, J. B. and Gade, P. A. (2012), Generational differences in work-related attitudes: A meta-analysis. *Journal of Business and Psychology,* 27(4), 375–394.

De Waal, A. and Jansen, P. (2013). The bonus as hygiene factor: the role of reward systems in the high performance organization. *Evidence-based HRM: a Global Forum for Empirical Scholarship,* 1(1), pp. 41-59.

Doyle, O. (2021). *How to Attract a Millennial & Gen Z Workforce | Occupop.* [online] Occupop.com. Available at: <https://www.occupop.com/blog/how-to-attract-a-millennials-gen-z-workforce> [Accessed 5 April 2021].

Dysvik, A. and Kuvaas, B. (2008). The relationship between perceived training opportunities, work motivation and employee outcomes. *International Journal of Training and Development,* 12(3), pp.138-157.

Edmonds, J., Hoops, A. and Schreffler, I. (2018). A Framework for Strategies in Employee Motivation. *Proceedings for the Northeast Region Decision Sciences Institute (NEDSI),* pp.1–19.

Fogliasso, C. E. and Linn, T. (2013). Job Satisfaction, Commitment, And Loyalty In The Workplace. *Leadership & Organizational Management Journal,* (1), pp. 106–119.

Halilbegovic, S., Celebic, N. and Idrizovic, A. (2018). Reward System Effects on Employees in Small And Medium Enterprises – Case of Federation Bosnia and Herzegovina. *European Journal of Economic Studies,* 7(2).

Jones, G. R., & George, J. M. (2011). *Essentials of contemporary management*. Boston, McGraw-Hill.

Karin Andreassi, J., Lawter, L., Brockerhoff, M. and J. Rutigliano, P. (2014). Cultural impact of human resource practices on job satisfaction. *Cross Cultural Management: An International Journal*, 21(1), pp.55-77.

Kreitner, R. and Kinicki, A. (2003). Organizational behavior. 1st ed. Salemba Empat: Jakarta.

Kurniawaty, K., Ramly, M. and Ramlawati, R. (2019). The effect of work environment, stress, and job satisfaction on employee turnover intention. *Management Science Letters*, pp.877-886.

Lloyd, J., Bond, F. and Flaxman, P. (2017). Work-related self-efficacy as a moderator of the impact of a worksite stress management training intervention: Intrinsic work motivation as a higher order condition of effect. *Journal of Occupational Health Psychology*, 22(1), pp.115-127.

Locke, E. A. (1976). The Nature and Causes of Job Satisfaction. *Handbook of Industrial and Organizational Psychology*, (1), pp.1297-1343.

Locke, E. and Schattke, K. (2018). Intrinsic and extrinsic motivation: Time for expansion and clarification. *Motivation Science*.

Mabaso, C. and Dlamini, B. (2018). Total rewards and its effects on organisational commitment in higher education institutions. *SA Journal of Human Resource Management*, 16.

Mickel, A. and Barron, L. (2008). Getting "More Bang for the Buck": Symbolic Value of Monetary Rewards in Organizations. *Journal of Management Inquiry*, 17(4), pp.329-338.

Omotayo, O., Pavithra, S. and Adenike, A. (2014). Compensation management and organisational commitment in developing economies: Indian perspective. *International Journal of Research in Management, Social Sciences & Technology*, 8(8), pp.1–15.

Pelta, R. (2019). *Generation Z in the Workplace: A Changing Workforce.* [online] FlexJobs Employer Blog. Available at: <https://www.flexjobs.com/employer-blog/generation-z-workforce/> [Accessed 5 April 2021].

Prakash Yadav, G. and Rai, J. (2017). The Generation Z and their Social Media Usage: A Review and a Research Outline. *Global Journal of Enterprise Information System*, 9(2), p.110.

Priya, D. and Eshwar, T. (2014). Rewards, Motivation and Job Satisfaction of Employees in Commercial Banks- An Investigative Analysis. *International Journal of Academic Research in Business and Social Sciences*, 4(4).

Reio, T. and Callahan, J. (2004). Affect, Curiosity, and Socialization-Related Learning: A Path Analysis of Antecedents to Job Performance. *Journal of Business and Psychology*, 19(1), pp. 3-22.

Rumpel, S. and Medcof, J. (2006). Total Rewards: Good Fit for Tech Workers. *Research-Technology Management*, 49(5), pp.27-35.

Ryan, R. and Deci, E. (2000). Intrinsic and Extrinsic Motivations: Classic Definitions and New Directions. *Contemporary Educational Psychology*, 25(1), pp. 54-67.

Sawitri, D., Suswati, E. and Huda, K. (2016). The Impact of Job Satisfaction, Organization Commitment, Organization Citizenship Behavior (Ocb) on Employees' Performance. *International Journal of Organizational Innovation*, 9(2), pp. 24–45.

Schroth, H. (2019). Are You Ready for Gen Z in the Workplace?. *California Management Review,* 61(3), pp.5-18.

Shafiq, M. and Naseem, M. (2011). Association between Reward and Employee Motivation: A Case Study Banking Sector of Pakistan. *SSRN Electronic Journal*.

Sia, S. and Appu, A. (2015). Work Autonomy and Workplace Creativity: Moderating Role of Task Complexity. *Global Business Review*, 16(5), pp.772-784.

Singhapakdi, A., Lee, D., Sirgy, M. and Senasu, K. (2015). The impact of incongruity between an organization's CSR orientation and its employees' CSR orientation on employees' quality of work life. *Journal of Business Research*, 68(1), pp.60-66.

Stiehl, S. K. et al. (2015). The role of motivation to lead for leadership training effectiveness. *International Journal of Training & Development*, 19(2), pp. 81–97.

Taylor, B. (2015). The Integrated Dynamics of Motivation and Performance in the Workplace. *Performance Improvement*, 54(5), pp. 28-37.

Tsede, O. and Kutin, E. (2013). Total Reward Concept: A Key Motivational Tool For Corporate Ghana. *Business and Economic Research*, 3(2), p.173.

Whitteberry, K., 2019. *Millennials vs. Gen Z In the Workplace: Hopes, Habits and Hangups.* [online] Iofficecorp.com. Available at: <https://www.iofficecorp.com/blog/millennials-vs-gen-z> [Accessed 5 April 2021].

Woolley, K. and Fishbach, A. (2018). It's about time: Earlier rewards increase intrinsic motivation. *Journal of Personality and Social Psychology*, 114(6), pp.877-890.

Wong, C., Hui, C. and Law, K. (1998). A longitudinal study of the job perception-job satisfaction relationship: A test of the three alternative specifications. *Journal of Occupational and Organizational Psychology*, 71(2), pp.127-146.

WorldatWork. (2015). The worldatwork handbook of compensation, benefits and total rewards. Hoboken, N.J.: Wiley.

The Hospitality and Tourism Sector: Some Observations on Challenges Facing Human Resources and Millennials and Gen Z Cohorts

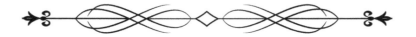

Jennifer Murphy, MSc.

Introduction

Before the impact of the COVID-19 pandemic on the global economic landscape, one of the largest and fastest-growing global industries, the Hospitality and Tourism sector, contributed an estimated $2.3 trillion to the global economy and accounts for over 109 million jobs worldwide (World Travel and Tourism Council 2017). This diverse and fast-paced environment offers prospective candidates opportunities to learn a variety of globally transferable skills. However, the demands of the industry are widely acknowledged to have a direct impact on retention of key talent and the ability to resource a great talent pipeline through succession planning, thus rendering Hospitality Human Resource professionals in a constant battle to attract and retain not only top talent but in recent times, successfully recruiting entry-level positions has presented significant challenges in and by itself (Salie & Schlechter, 2012). This is the case with Millennials and Gen Z.

Millennials and Gen Z have been particularly severely affected by the downturn in international and, subsequently, national, regional and local trade with government-enforced 'stay at home' pronouncements. Interestingly, a study by GlobalData (2020) noted that 48 per cent of Millennials (a.k.a. Gen Y) and 35 per cent of Gen Z are still very concerned about the risk of contracting COVID-19. Within these figures, Millennials are noted as willing to travel sooner and are less risk-averse than both Gen Xers and Boomers.

Recruitment and Retention

While recruitment and retention of key talent have always presented a challenge in this sector (Richardson, 2009), recent statistics show the Hospitality industry in Ireland enjoyed an approximate turnover €8.8 billion in 2018 (Tasc, 2019). With current trends within the sector placing increasing demand for labour, the cost of attracting high performers in an industry well known for lagging the market in terms of remuneration, is driving a review of work practices and benefits available to engage employees and reduce attrition (Riley, Ladkin, & Szivas, 2002). It is posited that HR professionals within the Hospitality sector are often faced with a decision to develop and manage all talent or focus on specific individuals, an even more complex challenge facing HR during the global COVID-19 pandemic. We have seen from other chapters in this book how Millennials and Gen Z cohorts place different emphases on their rewards aspirations. Thus, the unique demands of this industry present multiple barriers to investment in professional development in this regard, described some three decades ago as "dirty work", and the industry has numerous challenges to attract and then retain key staff (Mooney, 1999; Poulston, 2008).

From an employee perspective, Deery Leo Jago (2015) reported an industry characterised by low pay, unsociable working hours, dealing with often dissatisfied guests that leave workers feeling isolated and emotionally exhausted. This is a recurring theme from both Millennials and Gen Z. Notwithstanding the previous, recent research has identified that Gen Z workers do still view the industry in a positive light and believe it to offer an exciting and varied career with the added opportunity of travel incorporated, (Goh and Lee, 2018). From an owner's perspective, the rising costs of minimum wage in Ireland combined with recent changes in employment legislation regarding protected leave, the introduction of mandatory sick pay and other external economic factors such as VAT increases - not to mention a surge in a liability action, take a toll on even the largest of Hospitality operators and can endanger the sustainability of smaller, more rural enterprises who struggle to achieve basic occupancy levels whilst maintaining efficiencies and productivity in a predominantly seasonal industry (Kara, Uysal & Magnini, 2012). In research conducted by (Chiang and Shawn Jang, 2008) into the validity of the now revered Vroom's expectancy theory within the Hospitality sector, it was shown that Hotel workers perform best when intrinsically motivated. It is understood from the findings that Hotel workers do not expect to be rewarded in monetary terms yet enjoy the fulfilment of achievement and the satisfaction of accomplishment.

Managerial level Hospitality professionals proactively manage their careers and actively seek employment opportunities, which will enhance and develop them professionally. Failure of HR professionals to strategically plan for development and progression may result in the expense incurred to recruit and train a relevant comparator.

Research has shown that Hospitality professionals are thought to be broadly intrinsically motivated (Chiang and Shawn Jang, 2008; Louden, 2012); therefore, the opportunity to enhance current competencies and develop new skills is an inherent feature of cultivating commitment from employees. Unsurprisingly, the relationships between employees and their direct line managers also feature heavily in the positive connection with the organisation, with trust and autonomy playing a significant role in overall employee satisfaction levels. The evidence from the above research suggests that employees, who perceived their role as containing challenging elements, had higher levels of job satisfaction and organisational commitment. While compensation was essential to the participants of this research, it was widely acknowledged that remuneration and benefits alone, would in no way encourage talented employees to remain indefinitely with an organisation that failed to invest in their career progression. This is further compounded by the opinion of Gen Z and Millennial workers who value work-life balance above remuneration (MacGiolla Bhuí, 2020).

Baum (2008) discusses the unconventional suite of skills required from employees within the Hospitality sector, which differentiates it from other industries. The guest experience ultimately drives success in this sector; consumers have high expectations and little tolerance for error. Hospitality professionals, therefore, need to constantly utilise a combination of technical and interpersonal skills in a highly pressurised and often unrelenting environment, hence the emotional labour demands placed on employees is often a heavy burden to bear. Having an understanding of the complexities of this industry is imperative to designing the management of talent in this regard. More recently, Vicente (2015) discusses the importance of acknowledging the unique nature of this industry, the demands it places on employees and the relatively poor benefits and remuneration offered as the key to determining the strategic direction of effective talent management in Hospitality.

Interestingly, deCharms (1968) concur with McClelland (1965) and Maslow (1943) in discussion on the importance of autonomy, power and sense of achievement for job satisfaction and a sense of fulfilment to be cultivated within employees. A level of trust to complete a task to a satisfactory level is an essential element of employee motivation that links to retention.

Another distinct challenge presented is due to the fact, much of the customer-service based roles within Hospitality are highly transferrable to other industries, often offering better working conditions and reward structures (Baum, 1995; Riley, 1996). However, there is possibly one distinct exception, that of Chefs. Research into this division of employees' shows that Chefs and, in particular, Executive Chefs often consider their work "a calling" as distinct from "just a job". Their desire to perform to high standards and demonstrate innovation and creativity is derived from a deeply ingrained passion for their work (Lyubomirsky et al. 2005).

Retention/ Turnover / Attrition

Retention of employees is inherent to successful organisational performance, the phenomenon of which is somewhat under-researched (Vasquez 2014), yet a stable workforce contributes to the overall improvement of organisational performance. It is imperative that Organisational Leaders understand the core beliefs and values of this cohort if the objective is to adequately retain this talent pool and offer challenging careers. Millennial and Gen Z workers care deeply about the environment and place explicit value upon an organisation's attitude to environmental issues, so much so that a recent survey of the Millennial and Gen Z global workforce cite this as their top concern both prior to and after the current pandemic,(Deloitte 2020). Corporate social responsibility policy, therefore, plays as much part as compensation and benefits to the decision-making process of this talent pool. Whilst the COVID -19 pandemic attributed to an unprecedented health and economic crisis, a recent survey of this population of the workforce uncovered a surprising statistic in relation to retention and turnover. The research shows that this group of the labour pool now find the prospect of remaining with an employer for up to five years much more appealing than before (Deloitte Global Millennial Survey 2020). Previously, Millennial and Gen Z talent made no secret of their intention to change organisation after approximately two years of service. This would be in complete contrast to what Hartman and Yrie (1996) describe as the "hobo effect", whereby engagement activities and reward structures are often insufficient to create the commitment levels organisations crave. This is further compounded by the prevalent attitude of the Millennial and Gen Z workforce, for whom a long-term career with one organisation was not the norm. A major frustration for organisations in the Hospitality sector is the transient nature of the industry, with seemingly satisfied employees leaving their positions to work for other organisations. Capellii (1999) cites this notion of "self-directed careers" as the reason for sudden or often abrupt changes in organisation or career moves outside of the industry altogether.

In research conducted by Hausknecht, Rodda and Howard (2009) into the reasons employees remain with an organisation, the top four grounds cited in a study of 25,000 employees at varying levels within organisations were, firstly, job satisfaction, secondly extrinsic rewards, thirdly, constituent attachments and lastly organisational commitment. Research has consistently shown that job satisfaction is deeply entrenched as a motivational factor, regardless of the level of an employee. In much earlier research, Herzberg et al (1957) highlighted that, where a deficit of motivational factors occur, employee focus shifts towards hygiene factors, which create employee dissatisfaction. Furthermore, the importance of organisational commitment, the alignment of employee contribution, effort, belief in, and ultimately, the desire to achieve organisational goals is discussed extensively by Griffeth et al (2000). Retention of employees begins with the leaders within the organisation, and my experience as a Human Resources strategist confirms that employees should be motivated and developed, so they remain invested and committed to the organisation.

Not all turnover is problematic. Sometimes it is necessary if the person and the organisation do not share the same values, this can lead to frustration on both sides. Wallace and Gaylor state that "functional turnover is when low performing individuals are replaced by higher-performing individuals" (2012, p.12), while on the contrary, dysfunctional employee turnover is when "high performing individuals are replaced by weaker staff causing the remainder of the staff to work harder" (Wallace & Gaylor, 2012) and one area highlighted is that of talent management.

Walsh and Taylor (2007) and Sturman (2003) discuss the financial impact of turnover within the Hospitality sector and, again, note the disruption caused to team morale when turnover is high. The economic cost of replacing an experienced employee versus retaining a stable, productive workforce can be a major challenge for the Hospitality industry. Recruitment fees and training costs in conjunction with the time required for a new employee to begin actively contributing to the organisation can run into thousands of Euro. Therefore, to reduce employee attrition, it is imperative that the recruitment and selection practices are well planned and executed, and retention strategies are built into the core strategy.

As discussed by Boxall (2013), the basis of alignment between organisational goals and individual employee performance begins with compatibility between the candidate and the role specification. Consequently, it is vital that critical roles are identified and the talent pool managed accordingly. Typically, critical roles are identified as high strategic impact positions and those considered to have rarity.

Walsh & Taylor (2007) discuss the negative impact on Hospitality industries, in particular when employee turnover is high. High employee turnover can damage the reputation of the organisation and make it less attractive to the labour market candidates. One can make a direct connection between high employee turnover, lower team morale and increased stress on the remaining team. Often, this element of transient workers can leave a sense of instability among teams which can damage both the internal and external guest.

Recruitment and selection, the most fundamental part of the talent management process, consisting of attracting, selecting, rewarding and developing the talent pool, it has a far-reaching effect on overall organisational goal achievement (Keating & Harrington, 2003). Employers are dealing with a new generation of human capital (Cappelli 2019 & Solnet, Kralj and Kandampully, 2012). It is important to note that generational differences also effect motivational factors within the workplace. Thus, recruitment as part of a solid talent management strategy must endeavour to understand how to reach and attract the millennial and Gen Z labour pool.

Definitional Issues with the Term 'Talent Management'

Nijs et al (2014) have defined talent as 'the systematically developed and innate abilities of individuals that can be deployed in activities they enjoy and find important and in which they want to invest energy'.

Since the mid-1990s, talent management has become one

of the most popular terms used within organisations yet; the definition of talent management remains somewhat undetermined. One stream of thought cites developing talent as an organisational mindset, yet lack of concrete definitions and solid defined practices were concerns raised from the research, (Lewis & Heckman 2006 and Al Ariss et al 2014). However, the evidence suggests, it is widely accepted that the term talent management encompasses the strategic identification, attraction, acquisition, development and retention of high performing and high potential individuals; the intention being, to maximise employee contribution through effective engagement in roles that motivate and lead to high performance results (Farndale, Scullion & Sparrow 2010).

Determining the true meaning of talent management can identify human capital as both a resource and also a strategic competitive advantage essential to the delivery of organisational goals (Capelli 2008 & Collings 2012).

Approaches to Talent Management

The McKinsey Consultant Group first coined the term, "The War for Talent" almost two decades ago (Michaels, Hadfield-Jones & Axelrod, 2001). Organisations often differ in their talent management strategy with some preferring to focus on specifically targeted employees while other organisations adopt a more holistic approach to the inclusion of all employees as part of the talent pool (Lewis & Heckman 2006). Many organisations will refer to outstanding employees as high performers or employees demonstrating high potential, and will then focus talent management activities around harnessing and cultivating that talent, resulting in these employee groups often being selected for development opportunities (Blass 2007; Collings and Mellahi, 2009).

Urbanocova and Vnouckova (2015) looked to the philosophy of talent management and suggested that the manner in which an organisation conceives of, and views talent largely determines how it will strategise talent management. They identified the importance of organisational culture. They saw two fundamental differences to understanding talent management as a concept; individualistic or western cultures, and an achievement that can be trained and nurtured in eastern cultures. They assessed the talent management philosophies developed by Meyers and van Woerkom (2014), which developed four categories HR should concentrate on, as seen in the following, figure 1.

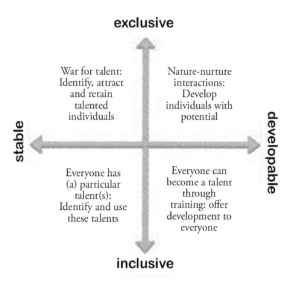

Figure 1. - Talent Management Philosophies. Source: Meyers and van Woerkom (2014) in Urbanocova and Vnouckova (2015)

Lepack & Snell (1999) discuss the notion of talent as having both uniqueness and being of value to an organisation. It is posited that individuals who are difficult to replace either due to labour market restrictions or, on account of working in a specialist role, are therefore unique. Employees who possess the ability to contribute to the delivery of organisational goals and improving competitive advantage in the market, are considered valuable (Lepack & Snell 2002). While organisations adopt their approaches to talent management, the literature offers multiple streams of thought in relation to what a robust talent management system consists of. The overarching concept involves strategic succession planning through effective development of high performers in crucial roles (Lewis & Heckman 2006), critical role identification is a crucial element as stated by Collings and Mellahi (2009) whereas, it is suggested by (Vaiman, Scullion, & Collings, 2012) that utilisation of HR data analytics is the leading edge in talent management and holds the key to employee performance and organisational goal alignment.

Watson (2008) has enumerated three distinct components of talent management which include:

- Talent selection
- Talent development
- Talent retention

Talent management then involves a strategic approach, and HR must look to understanding the purposeful and core activities involved. These include; who will these activities target and benefit and what are the implications in either having or not having a talent management protocol and schedule.

Components of a Talent Management System

Over the past few decades, research has focussed on the design, implementation and operation of talent programmes within organisations, but some industries display a lack of clarity on certain aspects (Macfarlane and Moss, 2013; Tarique and Schuler 2010). For example, in the context of the hospitality sector in Ireland, there is very high volumes of staff turnover compared to, the financial services industry.

The talent management system can be understood as a strategic process to encourage high potential and high performing employees to achieve their maximum level of productivity and efficiency whilst creating loyalty to the organisation. A talent management system provides an organisation with a framework to effectively develop its team. Often the components include training, engagement initiatives, performance related bonus packages, appraisals and career progression.

Gandz (2006) highlights the importance of not only upward development but also horizontal progression, which can enhance the skillset in preparation for future promotional opportunities. Giving equal importance to each aspect of the talent management system, it is considered to be a more holistic and organic development journey.

Firstly, a solid talent management system needs to have clearly identified the pivotal roles of the organisation. Pivotal roles being those that have a high impact on the guest directly and therefore have the potential to enhance or diminish the guest experience. Without a critical analysis of these roles, it would be impossible to successfully identify the candidate attributes required to assume the position and then deliver the organisational objectives of that role. Boxall (2013) argues that the human capital of an organisation should have both the capability to fulfil role requirements both now, static fit and into the future, dynamic fit. A workforce that possesses the knowledge, skills, and abilities to meet current needs and the flexibility to adapt as the organisation requires is the ultimate goal of a talent management system. Although the term and processes may have evolved somewhat, the similarities are undeniable even in the most modern organisation. The objective of managing talent in the simplest terms being to attract, motivate, retain and reward high performing and high potential individuals with the absolute intention of creating strategic competitive advantage, all whilst creating loyalty and long-term commitment, a precious commodity in Ireland's current tight labour market.

As discussed by Kwiecień, (2005), the most popular components of a successful talent management system are believed to consist of coaching and mentoring, organisational development programs, individual training and development and 360-degree feedback. Schiemann (2014) highlights the correlation between talent management and the talent life-cycle.

From initial attraction and acquisition of employees right through to development and retention resulting in an adequately resourced talent pool being the objective and return on investment for organisations.

The structure of a Talent Management System can be closely linked to the early eighties American phenomenon of a "High-Performance Work System" (Maślanka-Wieczorek, B. 2014). Such systems involve a combination of work-flow systems, incentivisation practices and reward structures to create employee engagement, connection with organisational goal achievement and ultimately career progression, for the organisation. The process should evoke commitment, retention, increased performance and improve competitive advantage.

The Role of HR

Often, training and development can be viewed as a cost as opposed to an investment. However, this stream of thought requires a paradigm shift, particularly in the Hospitality sector, if attracting and retaining top talent is a priority. Throughout this pandemic, Hospitality has taken arguably the most significant economic impact compared to other industries. Faced with lengthy closures and slow, heavily restricted measures when permitted to reopen, this has been detrimental to the industry's image as a secure career path. The research has consistently shown, the link between a culture of workplace learning, training and development have a positive impact on organisational outcomes (Johnson et al 2019).

Conversely, it is argued (Watson et al 2002, and Nolan 2002), that training and professional development costs pose a considerable barrier, particularly in smaller organisations. It is prudent to adopt an exclusive talent management system whereby only a few are selected for development. Notwithstanding, it is undeniable that in this constantly evolving Hotel industry where customer expectation is becoming increasingly more demanding, investment in employees is not only necessary but vital if organisations are to maintain or improve their market position (Gusain, 2017).

Whilst there once may have been a perception of talent management being the responsibility of Human Resource practitioners, successful talent management structures assert a portion of accountability to all of the leadership team for the collective management of talent (Morton 2004). In agreement with this stream of thought, Vicente (2015), cite an inclusive talent management system as a practical approach, considering the entry-level positions as part of the overarching goal of people development and succession planning.

Organisational leaders should actively train and develop management teams to empower and equip them with the necessary skills required to fulfil more senior roles in the future. This approach will assist in building reciprocal organisational commitment.

Scott & Revis (2008) further encourage employee investment, citing it as imperative to a customer-facing industry. It is arguable that engagement cascades through the organisation, and the cultivation of respectful, trustworthy and empowering environments is fundamental in creating the psychological contract. To create a team focused on a common goal and thus harness innovation, creativity and productivity through the effective engagement of employees at all levels of the organisation is akin to building a community of like-minded individuals who are as invested in achieving organisational outcomes in much the same manner as they would their personal goals (Garavan, Carbery, and Rock, 2012).

Conclusion

Watson (2008) urges organisations to be mindful of the reputational damage caused to the industry when talent is mismanaged and thus exits the business. Furthermore, it is crucial to acknowledge an abundance of talent available within the Hotel sector. Nonetheless, the literature points strongly to, a failure in cultivating professional relationships and enhancing development will result in extreme difficulty attracting and retaining top talent to the industry into the future. This may never be more so than in the current grip of this pandemic, as Hospitality faces such acute challenges and a gruelling recovery lies ahead. On the one hand, many Millennials and Gen Zers were employed in Hospitality and lost their jobs or were furloughed and, on the other, when we return to some sense of 'normalcy' (whatever that may be), one wonders if these cohorts will want to return to their previous roles. It is harrowing to watch the continuous vilification of Hospitality throughout the handling of this global pandemic. Arguably, reputable organisations that have spent and continue to spend tens of thousands of Euro on COVID-19 compliance measures operate some of the safest environments when compared to other industries such as meat factories, as one example. The image of Hospitality has been tarnished, rendering the attraction of top talent the biggest challenge for Human Resource practitioners. The much-discussed disadvantages of choosing a career in Hospitality are now, more than ever, in need of redress if the industry is to not only recover, but place itself in a position of being an industry of choice for the discerning Millennial and Gen Z.

Several commentators such as and Gelens et al, (2013) note that a clear definition of talent and, more specifically, talent management must be developed before an effective strategy can be put in place. This is particularly the case with Millennials and Gen Zers. Furthermore, it must be embraced and understood by the management team that 'one size does not fit all, as we have seen in the literature in this chapter and from my colleagues in this book. Sabuncu and Karacay (2016) suggest that HR departments should concentrate on ensuring the competitive advantage of an organisation by identifying and harnessing efficiency and productivity from employees (Gallardo-Gallardo and Thunnissen, 2016). The more 'talented' staff should be courted, and a culture of loyalty developed where talented staff feel genuinely recognised and rewarded. Having reviewed the literature, it is clear, more awareness is required concerning precisely how to attract, manage and retain the new generation of workers, namely the Millennial and Gen Z talent pool. For these individuals, flexibility, ample feedback, work-life balance, development opportunities and environmental responsibility hold significant value and organisational commitment is not naturally considered a priority. We still do not know enough about why this division of the labour market is so swift to change employers or move out of the sector altogether. Therefore the purpose of this research is to examine the reasons most commonly cited and identify trends or patterns which may assist the industry in reducing employee attrition.

References and Suggested Reading

Al Ariss, A., Cascio, W.F. and Paauwe, J., (2014). Talent management: Current theories and future research directions. Journal of World Business, 49(2), pp.173-179.

Alexander, J.A., Bloom, J.R. and Nuchols, B.A., 1994. Nursing turnover and hospital efficiency: an organization-level analysis. Industrial relations: a journal of economy and society, 33(4), pp.505-520.

Allen, D.G., Bryant, P.C. and Vardaman, J.M., (2010). Retaining talent: Replacing misconceptions with evidence-based strategies. Academy of management Perspectives, 24(2), pp.48-64.

Baum, T. (2006). Human resource management for tourism, events, hospitality & leisure. 1st ed. London: Thomson.

Baum, T. (1995), Managing Human Resources in the European Tourism and Hospitality Industry: A Strategic Approach, Chapman and Hall, London.

Baum, T. (2007). Human resources in tourism: Still waiting for change. Tourism Management, 28(6), pp.1383-1399.

Baum, T. (2008), "Implications of hospitality and tourism labour markets on talent management strategies", International Journal of Contemporary Hospitality Management, Vol. 20 No. 7, pp.720-729,doi:10.1108/09596110810897574.

Broeck, A., Vansteenkiste, M., Witte, H., Soenens, B. and Lens, W., (2010). Capturing autonomy, competence, and relatedness at work: Construction and initial validation of the Work-related Basic Need Satisfaction scale. Journal of Occupational and Organizational Psychology, 83(4), pp.981-1002.

Bobek, Alicja and Wickham, James., (2015). Employment in the Irish hospitality sector: A preliminary background report.

Boella, M. and Goss-Turner, S., (2020). Human Resource Management

In The Hospitality Industry. 10th ed. New York: Routledge, p.57.

Boselie, P. and Thunnissen, M. (2017). Talent Management in the Public Sector. Oxford Handbooks Online.

Boxall, P., (2013). Mutuality in the management of human resources: assessing the quality of alignment in employment relationships. Human Resource Management Journal, 23(1), pp.3-17.

Capelli, P. (2009), "Talent on demand: managing talent in an age of uncertainty", Strategic Direction, Vol.25No.3,doi:10.1108/sd.2009.05625cae.001. [Accessed 11 Aug. 2020].

Cappelli, P. (2019). Your Approach to Hiring Is All Wrong. [Online] Harvard Business Review. Available at: https://hbr.org/2019/05/recruiting [Accessed 11 Aug. 2020].

Chambers, E. (1998), "The war for talent", The McKinsey Quarterly, Vol. 1.

Chiang, C. and (Shawn) Jang, S. (2008). An expectancy theory model for hotel employee motivation. International Journal of Hospitality Management, 27(2), pp.313-322.

CIPD. (2014) 'Employee Turnover and Retention' [Online]. CIPD. Available from: http://www.cipd.co.uk/hr-resources/factsheets/employee-turnover-retention.aspx [Accessed 5 Feb. 2020].

CIPD. (2018). Employee Turnover & Retention | Factsheets | CIPD. [online] Available at: https://www.cipd.ie/knowledge/hr-fundamentals/resourcing/turnover-retention-factsheet [Accessed 3 Feb. 2020].

Collings, D. (2014). Toward Mature Talent Management: Beyond Shareholder Value. Human Resource Development Quarterly, 25(3), pp.301-319.

Collings, D. & Mellahi, K. (2009) Strategic talent management: A review and research agenda. Human resource Management Review. 19, 304 – 313.

D'Annunzio-Green, N., Maxwell, G., Watson, S., Scott, B. and Revis, S., (2008). Talent management in hospitality: graduate career success and strategies. International Journal of Contemporary Hospitality Management.

Dalton, D. and Mesch, D., (1990). The Impact of Flexible Scheduling on Employee Attendance and Turnover. Administrative Science Quarterly, 35(2), p.370.

deCharms, R. (1968). Personal causation: The internal affective determinants of behaviour. New York: Academic Press

Deery Leo Jago, M. (2015) Revisiting talent management, work-life balance and retention strategies. International Journal of Contemporary Hospitality Management, 27(3), 453 – 472.

DeNisi, A. and Murphy, K. (2017). Performance appraisal and performance management: 100 years of progress?. Journal of Applied Psychology, 102(3), pp.421-433.

Farndale, E., Scullion, H. and Sparrow, P., (2010). The role of the corporate HR function in global talent management. Journal of world business, 45(2), pp.161-168.

Forsek, B., (2017). The definition of talent and the influence it has on the implementation of talent management practices in Irish hotels (Doctoral dissertation, Dublin, National College of Ireland).

Gallardo-Gallardo, E., Nijs, S., Dries, N. and Gallo, P. (2015). Towards an understanding of talent management as a phenomenon-driven field using bibliometric and content analysis. Human Resource Management Review, 25(3), pp.264-279.

Gandz, Jeffrey. (2006). Talent development: The architecture of a talent pipeline that works. Ivey Business Journal. 1. 1-4.

Garavan, T., Carbery, R. and Rock, A. (2012). Mapping talent development: definition, scope and architecture. European Journal of Training and Development, 36(1), 5-24.

Gelens, J., Hofmans, J., Dries, N. and Pepermans, R. (2013). Talent management and organisational justice: employee reactions to high potential identification. Human Resource Management Journal, 24(2), 159-175.

Global Data, (2020).
https://www.googleadservices.com/pagead/aclk?sa=L&ai=DChcSEwi0m LXN0PbvAhVsgFAGHYyyB4oYABAAGgJkZw&ae=2&ohost=www.go ogle.com&cid=CAESP-D20hy-YmlhaXn5lbNx15znwQE2bRqfvz3m0I2k0gcqvFeK4JQKrL8l2CymFX 24qBzuWlj5gkPvgm4JRIoWRw&sig=AOD64_1LANW0epImF2mfsZ eSfzEKuWNMxQ&q&adurl&ved=2ahUKEwjxwK7N0PbvAhWfQhU IHZcmDUoQ0Qx6BAgCEAE&dct=1Accessed April 2nd 2021.

Goh, E. and Lee, C., (2018). A workforce to be reckoned with: The emerging pivotal Generation Z hospitality workforce. International Journal of Hospitality Management, 73, pp.20-28.

Griffeth, R., Hom, P. and Gaertner, S., (2000). A Meta-Analysis of Antecedents and Correlates of Employee Turnover: Update, Moderator Tests, and Research Implications for the Next Millennium. Journal of Management, 26(3), pp.463-488.

Gusain, N. (2017) Talent Acquisition vs Development: With a focus on leadership development programs. Cornell HR Review.

Gruman, J. and Saks, A. (2011). Performance management and employee engagement. Human Resource Management Review, 21(2), pp.123-136.

Festing, M. and Schäfer, L. (2014). Generational challenges to talent management: A framework for talent retention based on the psychological-contract perspective. Journal of World Business, 49(2), pp.262-271.

Hartman, S. and Yrle, A., (1996). Can the hobo phenomenon help explain voluntary turnover?. International Journal of Contemporary Hospitality Management, 8(4), pp.11-16.

Hausknecht, J., Rodda, J. and Howard, M., (2009). Targeted employee retention: Performance-based and job-related differences in reported reasons for staying. Human Resource Management, 48(2), pp.269-288.

Herzberg, F. (1968). Work and the nature of man. London: Crosby.

Hewitt Associates (2004), "What makes a best employer?", Insights and Findings from Hewitt's Global Best Employer's Study, Hewitt Associates, pp. 1-28.

Human Resource Management International Digest, (2012). Improving the hospitality sector. 20(3), pp.6-8.

Jeffrey M. Cucina, Kevin A. Byle, Nicholas R. Martin, Sharron T. Peyton, Ilene F. Gast, (2018) "Generational differences in workplace attitudes and job satisfaction: Lack of sizable differences across cohorts", Journal of Managerial Psychology, Vol. 33 Issue: 3, pp.246-264, https://doi.org/10.1108/JMP-03-2017-0115

Jehanzeb, K., Hamid, A. B. A. & Rasheed, A., (2015). What Is the role of training and job satisfaction on turnover intentions?. International Business Research, 8(3), pp. 208-220.

Johnson, K.R., Huang, T. and Doyle, A., (2019). Mapping talent development in tourism and hospitality: a literature review. European Journal of Training and Development.

Kaifi, B., Nafei, W., Khanfar, N. and Kaifi, M., (2012). A Multi-Generational Workforce: Managing and Understanding Millennials. International Journal of Business and Management, 7(24).

Kandampully,J. (2000),"The impact of demand fluctuation on the quality of service: a tourism industry example", Managing Service Quality: An International Journal, Vol. 10 No. 1, pp. 10-18, doi:10.1108/09604520010307012.

Kara, D., Uysal, M. & Magnini, V. P., (2012). 'Gender differences on job satisfaction of the five-star hotel employees'. International Journal of Contemporary Hospitality Management, 24(7), pp. 1047-1065.

Keating, M. & Harrington, D., (2003). 'The challenges of implementing quality in the Irish Hotel industry'. Journal of European Industrial Training, 27(9), pp. 441-453.

Kim, K., Watkins, K. and Lu, Z. (2017), "The impact of a learning organization on performance", European Journal of Training and Development, Vol. 41 No. 2, pp. 177-193, doi: 10.1177/001316448104100439.

Lee, C.C., Huang, S.H. & Zhao, C.Y., (2012). 'A Study on Factors Affecting Turnover Intention of Hotel Empolyees'. Asian Economic and Financial Review, 2(7), p. 866.

Lepak, D. and Snell, S. (2002). Examining the Human Resource Architecture: The Relationships Among Human Capital, Employment, and Human Resource Configurations. Journal of Management, 28(4), pp.517-543.

Lewis, R.E. and Heckman, R.J. (2006), "Talent management: a critical review", Human Resources Management Review, Vol. 16, pp. 139-54.

Louden, K., (2012). 'Preventing Employee Turnover'. Collector, 78(2), pp. 39-40.

Lyubomirsky, S., Kasri, F., & Zehm, K., & Dickerhoof, R. (2005). *The cognitive and hedonic costs of excessive self-reflection.* Manuscript submitted for publication.

MacGiolla Bhui, N., (2019). Mental Health for Millennials Vol.3 Galway: Book Hub Publishing

Maślanka-Wieczorek, B. (2014). Talent management and high performance work system. Journal of International Studies, 7(1), pp.102-108.

Maslow, A. (1943). A theory of human motivation. Psychological Review, 50, 370.

McClelland, D. C. (1965). Achievement and entrepreneurship: A longitudinal study. Journal of Personality and Social Psychology, 14, 389–392.

Mescher, S., Benschop, Y. and Doorewaard, H. (2010), "Representations of work-life balance support",Human Relations, Vol. 63 No. 1, pp. 21-39.

Mescher, S., Benschop, Y. and Doorewaard, H. (2010), "Representations of work-life balance support",Human Relations, Vol. 63 No. 1, pp. 21-39.

Melia, D., (2010). Critical Success Factors and Performance Management and Measurement: a Hospitality Context. School of Hospitality Management and Tourism, p.5.

Miscellaneous Provisions Act 2018

Michaels, E., Handfield-Jones, H. and Axelrod, B., (2001). The war for talent. Harvard Business Press.

Mooney, P., (1999). Keeping your best staff - A human resource challenge in a competitive environment. Dublin: Oak Tree Press.

Morton, L. (2004), Integrated and Integrative Talent Management: A Strategic HR Framework, Research Report R-1345-04-RR, The Conference Board, New York, NY.

Morton, L. (2005), Talent Management Value Imperatives: Strategies for Successful Execution, Research Report R-1360-05-RR, Conference Board.

Meyers, M.C. and Van Woerkom, M., (2014). The influence of underlying philosophies on talent management: Theory, implications for practice, and research agenda. Journal of World Business, 49(2), pp.192-203.

Mustafa Tepeci & Vivienne J. Wildes (2002) Recruiting the Best, Journal of Quality Assurance in Hospitality & Tourism, 3:1-2, 95-107

National Minimum Wage Act 2002.

Nijs, S., Gallardo-Gallardo, E., Dries, N. and Sels, L. (2014). A multidisciplinary review into the definition, operationalization, and measurement of talent. Journal of World Business, 49(2), pp.180-191.

Nolan, C. (2002), "Human resource development in the Irish hotel industry: the case of the small firm", Journal of European Industrial Training, Vol. 26 Nos 2/3/4, pp. 88 -99, doi: 10.1108/03090590210421969.

Poulston, J., (2008). 'Hospitality Workplace Problems And Poor Training: A Close Relationship'. International Journal of Contemporary Hospitality Management, 20(4), pp. 412-427.

Powell, M., Duberley, J., Exworthy, M., Macfarlane, F. and Moss, P., (2013). Has the British National Health Service (NHS) got talent? A process evaluation of the NHS talent management strategy?. Policy Studies, 34(3), pp.291-309.

Pwc.ie. 2020. Covid-19 And The Irish Hospitality Sector. [online] Available at: <https://www.pwc.ie/publications/2020/hospitality-sector-covid19-impact-and-options.pdf> [Accessed 3rd July 2020].

Richardson, S., 2009. Undergraduates' perceptions of tourism and hospitality as a career choice. Int. J. Hosp. Manage. 28 (3), 382–388.

Riley, M. (1996), Human Resource Management in the Hospitality and Tourism Industry, Butterworth Heinemann, Oxford.

Sabuncu, K.U. and Karacay, G., 2016. Exploring professional competencies for talent management in hospitality and food sector in Turkey. Procedia-Social and Behavioral Sciences, 235, pp.443-452.

Salie, S. & Schlechter, A., (2012). 'A formative evaluation of a staff reward and recognition programme'. SA Journal of Human Resource Management, 10(3), pp. 1-11.

Schiemann, W. (2014). From talent management to talent optimization. Journal of World Business, 49(2), pp.281-288.

Singal, M., (2015). How is the hospitality and tourism industry different? An empirical test of some structural characteristics. International Journal of Hospitality Management, 47, pp.116-119.

Solnet, D., Kralj, A. and Kandampully, J., (2012). Generation Y employees: An examination of work attitude differences. Journal of Applied Management and Entrepreneurship, 17(3), p.36.

Sturman, M. C. (2003). Utility analysis: A tool for quantifying the value of hospitality human resource interventions. Cornell Hotel and Restaurant Administration Quarterly, 44(2):106-116.

Tarique, I. & Schuler, R. S. (2010). Global talent management: Literature review, integrative framework, and suggestions for further research. Journal of World Business, 45(2): 122-133.

Tasc, (2019). Cherishing all equally in 2019: Inequality in Europe and Ireland.

https://www.tasc.ie/publications/cherishing-all-equally-2019-inequality-in-europe-a/ Accessed 3rd April 2021.

Tews, M. J., Michel, J. W. & Ellingson, J. E., (2013). 'The impact of coworker support on employee turnover in the hospitality industry'. Group & organization management, 38(5), pp. 630-653.

Towers Perrin (2003), The 2003 Towers Perrin Talent Report: Working Today: Understanding what Drives Employee Engagement, Research Report, Towers Perrin, Stamford, CT.

Towers Perrin (2005), Winning Strategies for a Global Workforce: Attracting, Retaining, and Engaging Employees for Competitive Advantage, Towers Perrin Global Workforce Study, Executive Report TP449-05, Towers Perrin, Stamford, CT.

Ulrich, D. (2016). HR at a crossroads. Asia Pacific Journal of Human Resources, 54(2), pp.148-164.

Ulrich, D., Younger, J., Brockbank, W. and Ulrich, M. (2012). HR talent and the new HR competencies. Strategic HR Review, 11(4), pp.217-222.

Van der Togt, J. and Rasmussen, T. (2017). Toward evidence-based HR. Journal of Organizational Effectiveness: People and Performance, 4(2), pp.127-132.

Vaiman, V., Collings, D. and Scullion, H. (2017), "Contextualising talent management", Journal of Organizational Effectiveness: People and Performance, Vol. 4 No. 4, pp. 294-297. https://doi.org/10.1108/JOEPP-12-2017-070

Varoglu, D. & Eser, Z. (2006). How service employees can be treated as internal customers in hospitality industry. The Business Review, 5(2): 30-35.

Vasquez, D. (2014). Employee Retention for Economic Stabilization: A Qualitative Phenomenological Study in the Hospitality Sector. International Journal of Management, Economics and Social Sciences 2014, Vol. 3(1), pp.1 – 17

Vicente, V.C. (2015), "The talent age", available at: https://core.ac.uk/download/pdf/61457245.pdf

Vroom, V.H., (1964). Work and Motivation. Wiley, New York.

Wallace, J. and Gaylor, K.P., (2012). A study of the dysfunctional and functional aspects of voluntary employee turnover. SAM Advanced Management Journal, 77(3), p.27.

Walsh, K. and Taylor, M. (2007). Developing In-House Careers and Retaining Management Talent. Cornell Hotel and Restaurant Administration Quarterly, 48(2), pp.163-182.

Walsh, K. & Taylor, M. S. (2007). Developing in-house careers and retaining management talent: What hospitality professionals want from their jobs. Cornell Hospitality Quarterly, 48(2): 163-182.

Watson,S.(2008), "Where are we now? A review of management development issues in the hospitality and tourism sector: implications for talent management",International Journal of Contemporary Hospitality Management, Vol.20 No.7, pp.758-780, doi:10.1108/09596110810897592.

Xanthopoulou, D., Bakker, A., Demerouti, E. and Schaufeli, W. (2009). Reciprocal relationships between job resources, personal resources, and work engagement. Journal of Vocational Behavior, 74(3), pp.235-244.

Wider Perspectives on Millennials and Gen Z

Gen Z and Environmental Action

"The Last of the One-Way Doors"

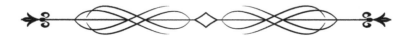

Dr. Phil Noone

Introduction

"The living world is a unique and spectacular marvel, yet the way we humans live on earth is sending it into decline"

— David Attenborough 2020:34

At the age of 93 years, the iconic voice of Sir David Attenborough continues his campaign for climate change (BBC Interview, 2020). He tells us that human beings have over-run the world, and we have just one last chance to embrace sustainability, reduce waste of power, food and plastic to reverse our environmental destruction. Gen Z are key drivers of this process because they are knowledgeable, caring and 'action-competent', as evidenced in the stories below. Furthermore, they are part of the younger generation that will see the consequences of both action and inaction in their lives.

Surfing

We were surfing. In Lahinch. A surfer's paradise on the Wild Atlantic Way on the West Coast of Ireland. Exhilaration from the white, sea-capped waves, later, we sit on the rocks, eating and watching other surfers glide and slice through the waves at speed. As we gathered up the rubbish, to our dismay, there were no recyclable rubbish bins. All rubbish was being disposed of in large plastic bags, destined for landfill. Born in 1998, my son Niall, is a Gen Z. A keen surfer, he is also environmentally aware and an environmental activist. He contacted Clare Country Council to highlight the issue and ask what action, if any, was planned to address it. In a speedy response, he was informed that Clare County Council are in the process of installing new environmentally friendly bins. Still waiting, but the campaign continues!!

This small example of individual responsibility can lead to collective action and demonstrate care and connectedness to nature and the wider world. This incident captures for me that young Gen Z's are interested in sustainability, able to adapt pro-environmental behaviours, and, most importantly, they are action-competent to spur on change. According to Gen Z, climate change is the greatest challenge in the next decade (Barliroglio 2019). Their concerns are well-founded. The planet is heating up and fast!!

Climate Change

The impact of human destruction as we release CO2 emissions into the atmosphere is devastating. Glaciers are melting. Sea levels are rising. Wildlife is scrambling to keep pace with a life that hangs in a balance while habits are being destroyed (Nunez 2019). A 2019 United Nations study estimates that up to one million plant and animal species face extinction within decades due to human activities. An October 2018 report from the World Wildlife Fund states that humanity has wiped out a staggering 60% of the world's animal population since 1970 (O'Sullivan 2020). The IPCC works on climate change, tracking these changes, and advocating a need for urgent behavioural change to avoid further environmental destruction (IPCC 2018). In 2018, scientists from the United Nations warned that if we could keep the rise in Greenhouse gas emissions at or below a level that caused the global climate to rise by 1.5 degrees compared to the pre-industrial levels, there was some hope of curtailing some of the worst impacts of climate change (O'Sullivan 2020).

Ireland's clean, fresh air and lush green landscapes, unspoilt natural habits cannot be taken for granted. The European Green Deal sets out a roadmap to ensure the EU's economy becomes sustainable (European Green Deal 2019-2024). Between 1990 and 2018, EU greenhouse emissions decreased by 23%, while the economy grew by 61%. The EU is the only major economy in the world to have legislation in place to cut greenhouse emission in line with the Paris Agreement.

To date, Ireland has failed miserably. We were committed to a legally binding EU target of reducing GHG emission by 20% on levels recorded in 2005 by 2020. We have only reduced these by 1%, and so face possible fines of hundreds of millions of Euro and not addressing the issues. The consequent damage to our planet. Temperatures in Ireland continue to rise, and it is projected that an average sea level rise of 0.5m to 1m by the end of the century. This, in combination with storm surge events, could result in as much as 1,000 km2 of coastal lands around Ireland being inundated by the sea. Admittedly, Ireland has defined a vision for a low-carbon economy, has identified 180 actions with a timeline for delivery in its new Climate Action

Plan (2019). Still, more significant action and funding are needed to achieve a decarbonised and sustainable future.

Although the issues that caused climate change are rooted in the behaviour of past generations, people such as Greta Thunberg, Isra Hirsi and Helena Gualinga, all Gen Z's and all environmental activists, are fighting for change.

Who are Generation Z?

Generation Z are the generation born after Millennials. This generation are born after 1996, and the oldest of them are now 22 years of age. They are born and raised with social media are digital centric, and their identity is influenced by technology. Because Generation Z has always had the internet, they are often called 'true digital natives', in comparison to Millennials. The latter adapted to the use of the internet during their young lives. A global study indicates that Generation Z are viewed as confident, optimistic with an 'action-competence' mentality that includes an interest in climate action, sustainability and environmental protection (Dabiji et al. 2020). A global survey with over 10,000, 18-25-year olds, across 22 countries indicated that 41% of respondent identified global warming as the most critical issue today, 84% identified that they would be willing to spend more on sustainable products, and 95% highlighted that they would be ready to change habits and lifestyle to combat global warming (Barliroglio 2019; Ostrander 2020).

Power of Social Media

The impassioned speech of Greta Turnberg on climate change is familiar to many. She used social media, particularly Instagram and Twitter, to spread her message. Jung et al. (2020) analysed her media use and messages, highlighting that by Feb 2020 she had 4 million followers on Instagram and 9.7 million followers on Twitter. This study shows that by the time the United Nations Action Summit on Climate Change was held on September 23rd 2019, her name was known worldwide. Her emotional plea to leaders of the world to urgently address climate change and preserve the natural work was broadcast worldwide.

The 'Greta-Effect' began to inspire other teenagers, Millennials and Gen Z's across the globe in climate activism. It is reported that 7.6 million young people gathered and rallied in projects for climate change across the world (Ostrander 2020). Social media allowed her to speak to the world directly in ways that were previously unknown to traditionalists (those born before 1948). Social media platforms offer Gen Z and Millennials a different form of communication and connection to others than ever before.

In Dara McAnulty's book, "Diary of a Young Naturalist" (2020), he shares with us how social media allows him to link and form connections with other like-minded nature lovers and environmental activists. His book, a fascinating read, chronicles his world as he moves from Spring to Summer, Autumn to Winter in his exploration of the natural world, his work as a conservationist and environmental activist. He is a 14-year-old, autistic, Generation Z, who describes in meticulous detail his deeply held connection with nature, his interest in preservation of the natural environment and enhancement of sustainability. He urges us to "create a safe space for nature in our gardens, especially during the winter months when the food is scarce. Caring for nature and ourselves can happen anywhere and everywhere, gardens filled with life, nature reserves, resting spots, feeding spaces, nourishing places" (McAnulty 2020: 180).

Where does Awareness of Nature come from?

In Dara's book, he tells us his love of nature was always present. He writes of the wonder and joy of the blackbird in spring: "the richness of the notes. I can pick them out, even from the most crowded air space. When the blackbird came, I could breathe a sigh of relief. It meant the day has started like every other. There was a symmetry. Clockwork. And each morning,

I'd listen and touch the shadows, not wanting to open the curtains and wake everyone up…So I listened and watched, the tiny movements of beak and body, the straight lines of the telephone wires, the thirty-second interval between verses" (McAnulty 2020).

From a very young age, I recall running about the fields, always exploring and fascinated with the wonders of nature. Both my parents were nature lovers, with a deep respect and interest in the preservation of the environment. My father was an environmental activist, relentlessly campaigning to convert a local rubbish dump into a picnic area, requesting to plant native trees along the village edge, never losing an opportunity to remind us that until the 1600's vast areas of Ireland were covered in forest, mainly ancient oak. An amazing legacy to leave to future generations and people living there today. But he was also a realist, trying to make a living and provide for his family. To my dismay, his nature sympathies did not stretch to crows and other birds as they descended with gusto on the blackcurrant bushes to feast on the juicy currants. We made jam. It was survival.

My early days were filled with nature-spaces. Each year, my excitement grew as we spotted and counted the spring cowslips peeping through new spring grass and the primroses snugly tucked away in the ditches, dancing in their early yellow glow. I recall the quells of laughter in anticipation of catching small frogs in the newly mowed meadow, slippy, smiley, green-coloured amphibians, with misshapen legs, or so I thought, and eyes so big, they seemed to devour their faces. I recall building a pond. A hole dug in a sheltered area of the garden with grasses, twigs, mosses to offer them comfort and protect their tender feet. I then spent hours erecting a fence from bits of timber and twigs to protect them and keep them enclosed. The simple wondering and imaginations of my nature days. And in the night, somehow, my captured frogs always manage to escape, no doubt released out of captivity by my Mother, allowing them freedom in the long grasses. Always hearing, touching, feeling, seeing, sensing what existed around me in that small farm space called home.

Research indicates that love of nature can act as influencers to green purchase, eco-labels and recycle habits. Song et al. (2019) explores Gen Z environmental concerns and their effects on their purchasing behaviours, indicating that eco-labelling has a positive impact on environmental attitude, concern, and green purchase behaviours, pointing to a greater awareness of eco-behaviour amongst Gen Z.

Results of an English survey, conducted with a representation sample of 24,204 people, provides strong support for the argument that people who have a greater appreciation of the natural environment and spend more recreational time in nature are reported to adapt greater environmentally friendly behaviours and pro-environment lifestyles (Alcock et al. 2020). Awareness of the environment comes in unexpected ways. Only yesterday, I was glancing through an Aldi leaflet that was pushed through the letterbox. Idly flicking through its pages. It was advertising back to school items. On turning to the back of the leaflet, I was delighted to see a campaign to reduce our carbon footprint. This was explicitly addressed to children and parents, recommending packing lunch in reusable bags, using a water bottle that can be refilled, reusing paper and packaging for fun crafts and recommending asking an adult about starting a herb or vegetable garden. In addition, it stated that 87% of their core range is recyclable, 850 tons of packaging is recyclable, that as a company, they removed 400 tonnes of plastic from their core range of products, 13.7 million milk cartons are made from fully renewable plant-based material. In addition, they planted 31,000 native hardwood trees and will plant a further 69,000 trees as part of phase 1 of their Tree Planting Project. I have no vested interest in any supermarket, but I am impressed. There was also an eco word search on the page, with words such as plant, green tree, ocean, eco, carbon, and recycle to locate. Simple but effective. It gives me hope. This leaflet is directed at parents and children. But if it is lying on the kitchen table and parent discuss its contents, and young people do the word search, the conversation has begun. With small steps, everyone can play a valuable role in adapting friendlier environmental habits and lifestyle change.

Other interesting environmental projects are taking place in Ireland today. While chatting recently to fellow author Cathy Fitzgibbon, I was enthralled to hear of a project involving the adoption of Bee Hives, where local beekeepers facilitate adopting a Bee Hive. As part of this process, the receiver is given locally produced honey and an opportunity to take an active role in talks and educational videos about bee-keeping. Initiatives such as these are innovative. They lead to greater awareness and understanding of the interconnected nature of human beings to our planet and the natural world around us. As Attenbborough (2020:220)) tells us, we must "rewild the world" and restore its biodiversity. Leading to an enrichment of our physical, emotional and mental health (Noone 2019), even more, important now as we learn to navigate the new world of global pandemic Covid 19.

Hiking

About two weeks ago, while hiking in Árainn Mhór in Donegal, I witnessed a different incident that stopped me in my tracks, an actual spur of the moment reaction towards the environment and the animals who live there. A Millennial act of kindness.

Towards the end of a 16 km hike, we passed an area of untamed briars and scrubland. We stopped. Listened. A bleating sound came from the tangled mess. A distress call. A cry for help. Within the blink of an eye, my daughter, Clíona, a Millennial, jumped the wall and ran to the brambles to see what unfortunate animal was caught, crying for help. I followed. By the time I reached the spot, Clíona was scrambling in the bushes, peering into the brambles. She stood. Her bare arms scratched from her efforts. Her laughter echoing in the barren landscape. It was an Irish goat or 'gabhar' in Irish. He wasn't trapped at all. But happily munching some tasty leaves. They are fantastic indigenous creatures, critically endangered and only found in remote mountain regions, mainly roaming in feral herds. The bleat of the goat is not commonly heard today unless when hiking in remote areas of the landscape. Another reminder of the preciousness of our Irish landscape, reinforcing the need to perverse its animals and wildlife.

The instinct to save a trapped animal, protect, and care for nature and its animals was at the forefront of this Millennials thoughts. Offering hope! I suggest that employers need to gain a deep understanding of Millennial and Gen Z culture to offer work-spaces that excite and challenge, to include a collective focus on environmental issues, innovate policies, a most importantly, a need to listen, to understand, to collaborate and work in partnership with these incredibly vibrant, dynamic young people.

Perhaps, it indicates that we are, as O'Sullivan reminds us, an incredible species, with technological and medical advances, space exploration, our achievements endless. A documentary filmmaker and ocean conservationist, he suggests that our potential, our abilities and achievements perhaps have been missing from the narrative of climate change (O'Sullivan 2020).

Perhaps, we need to listen to the music in our hearts, the earth's music, the planet, our environment, our world. We need to go deep within ourselves to hear it, to be still, to listen and allow the love we experience to flourish, to expand, so that we all adopt pro-environmental behaviour from now on and create a home for ourselves that is deeply, profoundly connected to nature and the natural world.

Conclusion

It is easy to complain, to blame everyone else, the government, the schools, the councils, the civil servants, corporations, multinationals etc. But I argue that like Gen Z and Millennials, we need to be action-competent. If single plastic is used in a supermarket, use your voice, write to the manager or company CEO to advocate for change, use your power, shop elsewhere! If politicians are not doing enough, write to them, write to newspapers, organise to have your voice heard. Why not plant a patch of wildflowers and watch the flutter of butterflies and hum of bees as they enjoy its bounty? Develop a vegetable garden, involving your children in the excitement of this project. I believe we have a shared social responsibility to stop waste and reduce CO_2 emissions. I conclude with the words of Sir David Attenborough, the most influential man on climate change the world has ever known:

"If we destroy the planet, we destroy ourselves
It's about saving us,
Stop Waste: Power, Food, Plastic,
The world is precious and needs to be cherished
This is the last chance
The last of the one-way doors."

— David Attenborough 2020.

References and Suggested Reading

Alcock I. & White M & Pahl S. & Duarte-Davidson R. & Fleming L. (2020) Association between pro-environmental behaviour and neighbourhood nature visit frequency and nature appreciation: Evidence from a nationally representative survey in England. *Environment International.* 136, 105441, 1-10.

Attenborough D. (2020) BBC Interview with David Attenborough. Available at: https://www.youtube.com/watch?v=2PRJL07-WK0 Accessed on 12/08/2020.

Attenborough D. (2018) *Adventures of a Young Naturalist.* Great Britain: Lutterworth Press.

Barliroglio E. (2019) *Generation Z fear climate change more than anything else. UN Climate Change Conference.* Available at: https://www.forbes.com/sites/emanuelabarbiroglio/2019/12/09/generation-z-fears-climate-change-more-than-anything-else/#5b3fabdf501b Accessed on: 13/08/2020.

European Green Deal (2019-2024) *Living Well Within the Limits of our Planet.* Available at: http://ec.europa.eu/info/strategy/priorities-2019-2024/european-green-deal_en   Accessed on 13/-8/2020

Dabija D. D. & Bejan B. M. & Dinu V. (2019) How sustainability orientated is Generation Z in retail: A literature review. *Transformations in Business & Economics.* 18(2), 140-155.

Dabija D. D. & Bejan B. M. & Puscas C. (2020) A qualitative approach to the sustainable orientation of Generation Z in retail: The case of Romania. *Journal of Risk and Financial Management.* 13 (152), 1-21.

Gaidhani S. & Arora L. & Sharma B. K. (2019) Understanding the attitude of Generation Z towards workplace. *International Journal of Management, Technology and Engineering.* 1X(1), 2804-2812.

Jung J. & Petkanic P. & Nam D. & Hyun-Kim J. (2020) When a girl awakened the world: a user and social message analysis of Greta

Thunberg. *Sustainability.* 122707, 1-15.

IPCC (2018) Global Warming of 1.5C: An IPCC special report on the impacts of global warming of 1.5C above pre-industrial levels and related global greenhouse gas emission pathways in the context of strengthening the global response to the threat of climate change, sustainable development and efforts to eradicate poverty. IPCC: Geneva.

Nunez C. (2019) Carbon dioxide levels are at a record high. Here's what you need to know. National Geographic. Available at: https://www.nationalgeographic.com/environment/global-warming/greenhouse-gases/ Accessed on 12.08.2020.

McAnulty D. (2020) *Diary of a Young Naturalist.* Dorset: Little Toller.

Noone P (2019) Finding Your Signature Strengths. Mental Health for Millennials. Vol 3. Mac Giolla Bhui N. & Noone P. (Editors). Pp 4-16.

Ostander M. (2020) In 2020, Millennials and Generation Z could force politicians to deal with Climate Change. The Nation, 23 August, 2019. Available at: www.thenation.com/article/archive/climate-change-yuth-public-opinion-election-2020/ Accessed on 4/08/2020.

O'Sullivan K. (2019) Stories from the Deep: Reflections on a Life Exploring Ireland's North Atlantic Waters. Dublin: Gill Books.

The Irish Government (2019) Climate Action Plan. Available at: http://www.gov.ie/en/pub;ications/5350ae-climate-action-plan/ Accessed on 13/08/2020.

Song Y. & Qin Z. & Yuan Q. (2019) The impact of eco-label on the young Chinese generation: the mediation role of environmental awareness and product attributes in green purchase. *Sustainability.* 11(973, 1-18.

United Nations Report (2019) Nature's Dangerous Decline: 'unprecedented', species extinction rates accelerating. Available at: https://www.un.org/sustainabledevelopment/blog/2019/05/nature-decline-unprecedented-report/ Accessed on 13/08/2020.

The Millennial and Gen Z Spaces:
#Connnectedness in a Time of Global Crisis

Susan McKenna, B.A., Dip. Soc Studies.

"Imagine being born in 1900. When you're 14 years old, World War I begins and ends when you are 18 with 22 million dead. Shortly after the "Spanish Flu" kills 50 million. Then at the age of 29, you survive the global economic crisis that started with the collapse of the New York Stock Exchange, causing inflation, unemployment and hunger. You're 39 when World War 2 begins, and it ends when you are 45 with 6 million+ Jews dead & around 75 million in total. There will be more than 150 million people dead before your 52nd birthday..."

— Anonymous.

The Global Pandemic of COVID-19

On December 31st 2019, Wuhan Municipal Health Commission in China reported a cluster of cases of pneumonia in Wuhan Hubei Provence. This was later updated to a novel coronavirus (hereafter called COVID-19). By March 11th 2020, the World Health Organisation proclaimed that the incredible speed and the severity of COVID-19 could be described as a world pandemic.

At the time of writing this chapter at the end of March 2021, we have a recorded 126 million cases worldwide, 2.77 million deaths and 233,000 recorded cases, with 4,651 deaths occurring here in Ireland (HSE, 2021). Thus, just over twelve months ago, we started to read and watch news reports informing us of people who were getting ill presenting with strange cases of flu-like symptoms. We didn't know it then, but our lives were about the change forever (Ang, 2020). The same way we went about our daily business was no longer safe, no longer routine. We had to find new ways of engagement, new ways of communicating, new ways of doing business. And this has mainly been the case with Millennials and Gen Z, as expressed by Liang, Ren, Cao, Hu, Qin et al., (2020).

The Suez Canal March 2021 Shipping Incident

We have been further reminded of just how interconnected the world is with a recent incident of a single container ship, that's right just one ship, becoming grounded in the Suez Canal in March 2021 which had globally catastrophic consequences.

As of March 28th 2021, as many as 321 ships are currently waiting in queue to transit through the canal. There are no detours from inside the channel at this point which is presenting substantial logistical problems. It's the second seemingly innocuous event in a distant land that has profoundly impacted the global economy. The figures are staggering. Who knew before this event that approximately 12% of the world trade volume passes through the Suez Canal. Just under $10 billion a day in cargo is handled, and 18,800 ships with a net tonnage of 1.17 billion tonnes passed through the canal during 2020, averaging 51.5 ships per day (CNN, 28.3.2021). The blockage has occurred in one of the world's busiest and most important waterways, resulting in unforeseen global supply chain shortages, with Lloyds List estimating the cost at $400 million per hour.

Onboard the containers are hundreds of thousands of technology items such as phones and tablets, laptops and MacBooks and home gym equipment and leisurewear – all favourites of both Millennials and Gen Z.

Information Overload: 'Globalisation' or 'Connectedisation'

Government and news sources have continually either contradicted each other in the reportage of events or have deliberately chosen and maintained a narrative. The already creeping distrust in formal political systems and news agencies has been further dented. As an example, the Daily Mail online portal ran a headline on 28.2.2020 that read, 'Mexican government admits the country's true COVID death toll is 321,059 – almost 60% higher than previously reported'.

Millennials and Gen Z were already choosing to be informed through their social media feeds as opposed to the more traditional platforms of, say, the 6 pm and 9 pm national news broadcasts by RTE here in Ireland, and this has profound implications for core agencies trying to disseminate 'real time' information to younger demographics. Indeed, in a recent Ypulse survey (2020), 27% of Gen Z and 26% of Millennials reported social media is their primary source for news – so almost a third with each, although this is changing. Thus, these generations were essentially informing themselves from peer networks – but with notable differences.

The Ypulse survey (2020) further reports that both generations were now less likely to say that they get their news only from social media, with Gen Z decreasing from 58% in 2019 to 49%, and Millennials dropping from 65% in 2019 to 50%. These are not inconsiderable drops. Additionally, Millennials are also more likely than Gen Z to get their news from other sources, including newspapers, websites for print newspapers, and news email updates. Gen Z, on the other hand, is more likely than Millennials to report they rely on word-of-mouth for news. Gen Z is also happy to break from tradition and move to new social platforms as news sources being far more likely than Millennials to use Instagram, YouTube, Snapchat, and the ever-growing TikTok, to get their news (Ypulse, 2020).

There was, and is, no doubt now that we are all connected throughout the world. Whether one terms this 'globalisation' or 'connectedisation' is of little importance now as it's academic mainly (Moreton, Arena and Tiliopoulos, 2019). In the real world, it's clear that a single occurrence in the remotest part of the world can profoundly affect the rest of us in a very new way. This is both terrifying and exhilarating, as seen by the two examples presented above.

Of course, there has been the threat of prominent 'massive' events such as nuclear war or nuclear leakage hanging over us all for decades. Still, it's the seemingly more minor events such as a random bat virus in rural China or ship grounding in the Suez Canal that are very different to come to terms with. How could such things become so globally catastrophic, so quickly? And, particularly so for Millennial and Gen Z populations who immediately saw many of their roles disintegrate, their identity questioned.

Understanding Millennials and Gen Z

Millennials are usually defined as having been born somewhere between 1981 to 2000 or from 1981 to 1999 or 1980 to 1995 (Twenge, 2006). As the reader, you can choose which band you find most appropriate. And, there's lots of exciting research on Millenial culture. It is proposed that Millennials desire a more frequent recognition than generations that went before them, and they tend not to measure their success necessarily by euros in the bank but opt, instead, to earn less at something they love to do rather than earn more at something they fundamentally dislike doing (Flippin, 2017). Millennials like experiences (MacGiolla Bhuí, 2018).

Gen Z includes all those born after 1996. Already, the impact of COVID-19 on both Gen Z's finances and careers is complex: Younger members are scrambling to get into online learning modalities and the oldest members of this generation, those turning 22 and 23, might well fare the worst economically, although many have at least some third-level qualifications. Entry-level employment has nosedived, and paid internships all over the globe have been cancelled or deferred. Gen Zers in the 20 to 24 age category may be found in disproportionate numbers in services industries which have been the most immediately and badly affected sectors. Gen Z was already becoming a risk-averse cohort pre-pandemic, but this process has been dramatically accelerated.

Millennials, Gen Z and the Internet

More and more a year on in the global pandemic, we see fundamental communication behaviour change across the Millenial and Gen Z landscapes in terms of how they choose to engage. For examples, the sharing of 'pics' and 'updates' has become an integral part of everyday life (Twenge and Campbell, 2015). However, this constant self-portrait phenomenon is beginning to show significant effects on peoples' thoughts and behaviours. But, how much of the sharing is what we might consider informative to peers?

Marie Boran, writing in The Irish Times (2.8.2018), reported the first-ever #selfie was posted on Instagram as recently as 2011, just a decade ago, and has gone on to become the most frequently used hashtag on the platform. "Selfie" had officially gained buzzword status just twelve months later, and in 2013 the Oxford English Dictionary gave it the honour of 'Word of the Year'. If one doubts how ubiquitous selfies have become, here's an interesting statistic. A 2013 survey of 3,000 individuals aged 18-24 found that every third picture taken is a selfie.

On top of this, we have the phenomenon of Internet 'memes'. A meme may be created deliberately by an individual or an agency (indeed, it is the 'go to' of advertising and marketing companies to create viral content). Memes can also be an accidental image, turn-of-phrase or concept that are circulated.

In both the cases of COVID-19 and the Suez Canal shipping incident, there are now memes generated on a minute by minute basis filling up the feeds of Millennials and Gen Z. What does this do to their sense of reality? How active are they in generating and sharing such memes themselves? How much is disinformation or misinformation?

References and Suggested Reading

Alberti, F. B. (2019). *A Biography of Loneliness: The History of an Emotion.* New York, NY: Oxford University Press.

Ang, Y. Y. (2020). When COVID-19 meets centralized, personalized power. *Nat. Hum. Behav.* 4, 445–447. doi: 10.1038/s41562-020-0872-3

BusinessInsider, (2021) https://www.businessinsider.com/boat-stuck-suez-canal-costing-estimated-400-million-per-hour-2021-3?r=US&IR=T Accessed 29.2.2021.

Courtet, P., Olié, E., Debien, C., and Vaiva, G. (2020). Keep socially (but not physically) connected and carry on: Preventing suicide in the age of COVID-19. *J. Clin. Psychiatry* 81:20com13370. doi: 10.4088/JCP.20com13370

CNN, (28.3.2021). https://edition.cnn.com/2021/03/27/africa/suez-canal-ship-refloat-attempt-intl/index.html Accessed 28.3.202.

Daily Mail, 28.2.2021.

Galea, S., Merchant, R. M., and Lurie, N. (2020). The mental health consequences of COVID-19 and physical distancing: the need for prevention and early intervention. *JAMA Int. Med.* 180, 817–818. doi: 10.1001/jamainternmed.2020.1562

Health Service Executive, (2021). COVID-19 Statistics. HSE.

Liang, L., Ren, H., Cao, R., Hu, Y., Qin, Z., et al. (2020). The effect of COVID-19 on youth mental health. *Psychiatr. Q.* 91, 841–852. doi: 10.1007/s11126-020-09744-3

MacGiolla Bhuí, N. (2018). The Search for self-identity and flow in the millennial space: Filtered incrementalism. Mental Health for Millennials, 14-22, Vol 2. Galway: Book Hub Publishing.

Miller, E. D. (2020). The COVID-19 pandemic crisis: the loss and trauma event of our time. *J. Loss Trauma* 25, 560–572. doi: 10.1080/15325024.2020.1759217

Moreton, S., Arena, A., and Tiliopoulos, N. (2019). Connectedness to nature is more strongly related to connection to distant, rather than close, others. *Ecopsychology* 11, 59–65. doi: 10.1089/eco.2018.0063

The Irish Times, (2.8.2018).

Twenge, J. M. (2006). Generation Me: Why today's young Americans are more confident, assertive, entitled--and more miserable than ever before. New York, NY: Free Press.

Twenge, J. M., & Campbell, W. K. (2010). The Narcissism Epidemic: Living in the Age of Entitlement. Atria Books.

Ypulse, (2020). https://www.ypulse.com/article/2020/07/20/gen-z-millennials-have-very-different-news-sources/

Comestible Connectivity in the Workplace

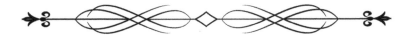

Catherine Fitzgibbon, MBus,
aka "The Culinary Celt"

"Food for us comes from our relatives, whether they have wings or fins or roots. That is how we consider food. Food has a culture. It has history. It has a story. It has relationships"

— Wiona Laduke.

Breaking Bread

Millennials take centre stage when it comes to food. This foodie generation has fundamentally changed the way food is created, served and delivered in the workplace by being part of a transformation age which has allowed them to disseminate information at speed making it important for employers to offer more transparency, consciousness and connectivity when it comes to their food offerings. Then just when we thought we'd figured out Millennials, Generation Z are now making an entrance into the workforce! This generational cohort have been exposed to what it means to be connected, transparent and conscious for all their lives, having grown up in an era where technology such as iPads, smartphones, and social media are the norm. With Generation Z being the up and coming workforce and game changers in relation to food it's important from the outset to recognise that 'connectedness' from inception sets them apart from previous generations.

As "Gen Z" transition into the workplace, Millennials are adapting in order to survive and collaborate with this new generation. In the world of food marketing, authenticity has become a core focal point. Millennial consumers were the first generation to make known their preference for authentic content whilst Generation Z are going further by making it clear that it's important for them to feel connected to brands and the people behind them. It's the reason that so many food brands have now made conscious decisions to make their marketing campaigns as true to life and as relatable as possible. One such example is the Happy Pear. Irish plant-based vegan chefs, Dave and Stephen Flynn, have achieved success by marketing their 'Happy Pear' brand in terms of being a movement to create happier healthier lifestyles in a community style environment that make people feel supported in their efforts to make change (The Happy Pear, 2020).

Culinary Connectivity WORKS!

Our attitudes may differ when it comes to nutrition. However, it's an undeniable primary fact that food is required to provide daily sustenance. Today's food-centric generations (Millennials and Generation Z) have elevated food to a new level given rise to more fully immersive food experiences at work. Being more food-focused at work than previous generations, both of these generational cohorts tend to put further emphasis on their food workplace offerings. In response to this, employers are beginning to realise the efficacy of healthy food in terms of productivity in the workplace. According to Short (2019), some companies now understand the importance of food as an enabler in retaining valuable employees, by providing a work environment conducive to wellness with food at the heart of the proposition. For instance, employees at the global tech company Google enjoy some terrific perks at work. Historically, Google employees appreciated perks such as paid maternity and paternity leave however Yang (2017) suggests that in more recent years they have highlighted workplace food and food education offerings as some of their most favourite perks at work. Bock

(2015) supports the view that Most of their food source offerings such as cafes, canteens and micro kitchens are strategically placed between different work teams with the goal being to connect them together by encouraging them to interact and collaborate. By creating these types of food spaces employers also positively encourage employees to leave their desk and interact with other work colleagues, whose workspaces are not nearby. A variety of free cookery classes and demonstrations which are offered as perks for employees, that were traditionally available on-site, have now moved online to connect remote staff working from home, allowing them to continue to bond with teammates whilst also enabling them to learn how to make new dishes. To that effect McNamee (2020) reported that after lockdown a lot of large corporate companies in both Ireland and abroad, wanted Ballymaloe Cookery School based in East Cork to run online cookalongs with their staff.

During the recent COVID-19 pandemic, which is still on-going, Kunthara (2020) highlights the fact that numerous companies worldwide such as Fitbit and Red Bull have increasingly embraced home delivery options by providing employer-subsidized, work-from-home boxes to for their employees You may ask yourself the reason why companies are pivoting and provide these fantastic workplace food offerings and food perks? Well, in a most cases the purpose of these perks is to help support staff during this challenging time and inspire a culture of innovative thinking.

Hungry for Knowledge

These two demographic cohorts' tend to face criticism over their commitment to the workplace. Brandished by Bhunjun (2018) as work-shy generations exhibiting "snowflake" tendencies, these young adults are reported as being more prone to taking offence and being thin-skinned compared to previous generations. On the contrary, recent data analysis by Fry and Parker (2018) from the Pew Research Center shows that Generation Z are the most diverse and highly educated generation. This remains evident when it comes to food as Millennials and Gen Zers are both demanding fresh, organic and sustainable food offerings. According to the Food and Agriculture Organization of the United Nations (2004) the previous selection of food that used to feed daily diets was limited, with 75% originating from just twelve plant and five animal species. Younger generations recognise that this widespread food consumption monotony and dependence on a narrow range of agricultural products may lead to health implications as well as increasing vulnerabilities on their food system, that currently appear to be under threat from climate change.

Millennials and Gen Z tend to take a holistic view when it

comes to their health. To this effect they place considerable emphasis on the importance of physical fitness, healthy eating, and mental well-being. When it comes to food, they want convenient and healthy options available to them. A recent Nielsen Global Health and Wellness Report (2015) discovered that Gen Zers are the most willing of all generations to pay a premium for healthy foods, such as all-natural, sustainable and GMO-free foods. In terms of nutritional choices, Gen Z are in favour of low-carb, high-protein foods, likely to consume plant-based products and are also more open to becoming vegetarian. Jed (2018) maintains that these dietary choices are primarily motived by health and environmental concerns with almost 80% of Gen Z planning to go meatless at least once or days per week.

Over the past two decades, social media has played a huge part impacting these younger generations. Due to these advances in technology the passage between Millennials and Gen Zers has accelerated intensely in terms of food. The fact that both generations have grown up with companies marketing to them largely through social media platforms, as much as every other advertising channel, makes them question authenticity more when it comes to the food they choose to eat. With the average attention span of this iGeneration being down four seconds from the attention span of millennials Reilly (2017), this youngest generation have adapted and developed more of a "Grab and Go" culture when it comes to food than the previous generations that have gone before them. For the past five years, Jack Kirwan founder and co-owner of the Dublin based Sprout & Co. has successfully been providing this type of healthy grab and go food offering to meet the needs of these food-centric generations. He maintains that technology has been a huge enabler of efficiencies in running the business successfully and he also understands the importance of transparency when it comes to sourcing ingredients (Bord Bia, 2017).

Whilst we are currently living and working in this era of COVID-19 it has also become apparent that these generations are starting to pay more attention to the science of food functionality, opting for more nutritional food sources that will help boost their immunity. According to recent Google searches immune-building foods, vitamins and minerals including vitamins C and D, elderberries and spinach are a selection of food source and vitamin search terms that are being researched for their immune potential.

Food Centrality at work

A study published by the Global Wellness Institute (GWI) in 2018 valued the workplace wellness market at a staggering $47.5bn (Kumar, 2018). Given the considerable time that employees spend in their jobs Quintiliani *et al.*, (2010) believe that workplaces now represent an influential setting for influencing dietary patterns. By extension these communal food consumption patterns highlight the influence of workspaces as being an important centre for shared food moments and experiences. I touched on the fact that we consume food differently when we're in the company of other people compared to when we eat alone in a recent publication titled "Millennial Culinary Curiosity: Generation Foodie Fuelling Generation Next" (Fitzgibbon, 2019).

The current COVID-19 pandemic has changed this traditional dynamic of workplace settings with employees now, more than ever, craving social connection. Pre-COVID-19, working from home was considered a top employee perk whilst now, in most cases, it's a requirement. With lockdown restrictions in place, various governments worldwide are making it compulsory for employees in non-essential workplace employees to work in homebased settings to help in their national efforts to reduce the COVID-19 virus number. Companies are becoming creative, finding unique ways to bring together and engage employees by way of food and it's centrality context in the workplace setting. Deloitte Australia has independently experimented in this idea of virtual socialising by way of meals shared with their virtual team members around a video conference meeting with no agenda. These brown bag lunch events have become increasingly popular enabling remote workers to take a break and engage with each other whilst mainstreaming flexibility. HR departments are also co-ordinating voluntary lunchtime Zoom video sessions for employees that allowed them to talk about things unrelated to work.

Recent research in understanding millennials highlights the priority they place on forging shared experiences using food and drink via their capturing and sharing of food moments (Bord Bia, 2014). Being digital natives having always known a life emphasised by shared connections Generation Z have embraced and further accelerated this concept. Furthermore, most of these Gen Zers are looking for food options at work that fit in with their core values. Thus, being inclusive and social food can help to bind work colleagues and generations together.

IncrEDIBLE Engagement

According to the global foodservice company Sodexo (2020), "the new 360-degree workplace food landscape is reshaping traditional approaches based on consumer insights and big trends transforming the way we work and live". Food is now an offering at work that a multitude of companies are building with employee participation. Unlike the traditional one-dimensional workplace food offerings which previously were enough to satisfy employees, these new 360-degree food landscape offerings are enabling employers to consider employee wellbeing, productivity and performance.

As the behaviours and perceptions of the new generation of employees have evolved, so too have their expectations when it comes to food in the workplace. Millennials and Generation Zers are used to a different standard of foodservice and expect this to be mirrored in their workplace food experience. Traditional lunch hours have become obsolete. Be it working remotely or in office settings, these new generations have one thing in common - they are looking for more flexible offerings that fit flawlessly into their lifestyles. When it comes to food, they expect the same level of convenience and choice that they receive outside the office environment.

COVID-19 has accelerated the need for employers to embrace solutions that support these changing workstyles and evolving expectations, with emerging innovations that bring new value to employees. Companies have been adopting innovative incentives to maintain productivity and engagement among their telecommuting staff. Perks related to food and drink, teambuilding and the use of technologies such as Zoom, Microsoft Teams, Google Hangouts have been embraced while HR departments are in the process of making ongoing adjustments and rethinking new approaches in terms of their company cultures.

Food has always been a social movement, by way of its

network of informal interactions between individuals, groups and organizations on the basis of its shared collective identity. The current COVID-19 pandemic workplace has globally accelerated food changes, allowing both Millennial and Gen Z generations to explore the world of 'Social Gastronomy', in terms of new and different approaches of acting and thinking when it comes to the collective food in the workplace space. We have seen social gastronomy in action with campaigns such as 'Feeding the Frontline Workers'. Clean Cut Meals, a Galway-based healthy food preparation and delivery company, in the West of Ireland is one of many food companies, having delivered free healthy and nutritional meals to medical and frontline staff at their workplaces during this crisis. With many of them working exhaustive hours during this global healthcare crisis it has left many of them with very little time to shop or cook. Then at the other end of the spectrum other catering and food businesses are serving at-cost meals to supply food-insecure residents in their communities.

Hurrah for Hyperlocal!

Having never known a world without a smartphone, Gen Z are hyper-connected (Powell, 2015). They are highly aware of what is happening around them on both a regional and global level making them both hyper-local and hyper-global. The recent Mitchell (2019) "OmniLocal Consumer Report" examined the new definition of local and the implications for brands. This research showed that 74 per cent of Millennial and Gen Z consumers do not consider geographic location when defining "community." Instead, more than half of these surveyed generations maintain that "local" is anywhere that they connect with others who share their same interests. For many Millennials and Generation Zers work is a central focus in terms of their shared values and interests. So, on this front it's important for employers to understand and embrace the 'Hyperlocal' concept when it comes to food, in order to satisfy employee expectations.

Deliveroo is a fantastic example of cutting-edge food company that appeals to these food-centric generations, having surpassed everyone in their niche food delivery platform. With operations in several global locations the company is currently valued at around $2 billion (Singh, 2019). Disrupting the traditional business models Singh (2019) proposes that Deliveroo combined the aggregator business model with the marketplace and logistics business model to create an all-new hyperlocal on-demand business model. By positioning the business as a hyper-local brand they can effectively offer a diverse premium range of local food via their network of global locations. The Covid-19 pandemic has helped to further shine a beacon of light on local produce and producers, with social media platforms trending hashtags such as #buylocal, #shoplocal and #supportlocal, reminding us all to help sustain work and local employment in our communities.

The Future of Food at Work

The future looks bright in terms of comestible connectivity in the workplace. Both Millennials and Generation Z have the potential to reset expectations impacting the future of the food. Raised to focus on the quality of food, whether it's fresh, clean, or nutritionally beneficial these younger generation employees are now becoming collaborators in the movement toward a better and more sustainable food future. They are leading the way by already making conscious choices aimed at driving positive impact for the good of the planet in their own lives whilst also influencing those around them. It will be important for employers to align their food offerings with these trends to meet this modern employee mindset.

> ... *"La nourriture est notre terrain d'entente, une experience universelle"*
>
> — James Beard.

References and Suggested Reading

Bhunjun, A. (2018) "What is the Snowflake Generation?", available at https://metro.co.uk/2018/01/10/what-is-the-snowflake-generation-7218112/, accessed at 21:40, 6th June.

Bock, L. (2015) "Work Rules!: Insights from Inside Google That Will Transform How You Live and Lead", Twelve.

Bord Bia (2014) "Understanding Millennials for Better Connections", available at https://horticultureconnected.ie/news/understanding-millennials-for-better-connections-part-3/, accesses at 16:42, 16th Sept.

Bord Bia (2017) Foodservice, Aviva Stadium, Dublin. "Irish Foodservice Channel Insights", available at https://www.bordbia.ie/globalassets/bordbia.ie/newsevents/speaker-presentations/speaker-presentations-2017/irish-food-service-directory/2017-irish-foodservice-channel-insights.pdf, accessed at 18:19, 4th August.

Fitzgibbon, C. (2019) "Mental Health For Millennials, (Vol 3)", Book Hub Publishing.

Food and Agriculture Organization of the United Nations (2004) "Building on Gender, Agrobiodiversity and Local Knowelege", available at http://www.fao.org/3/y5956e/Y5956E03.htm#ch1.1.1, accessed at 17:39, 18th June.

Fry, R. Parker, K. (2018) "Early Benchmarks Show 'Post-Millennials' on Track to Be Most Diverse, Best-Educated Generation Yet", available at https://www.pewresearch.org/social-trends/2018/11/15/early-benchmarks-show-post-millennials-on-track-to-be-most-diverse-best-educated-generation-yet/, accessed at 21:05, 12th June.

Jed, E. (2018) "Aramark Brings Gen Z Food Trends To Life On College Campuses Nationwide", available at https://www.vendingtimes.com/news/aramark-brings-gen-z-food-trends-to-life-on-college-campuses-nationwide/, accessed at 19:12, 20th June.

Kumar, S. (2018) Global Wellness Institute: Global Wellness Economy Monitor "Healthonomics: How Wellness is Merging With Other Industries As a Ubiquitous Economic Force", available at https://timesofindia.indiatimes.com/blogs/edge-of-evolution/healthonomics-how-wellness-is-merging-with-other-industries-as-a-ubiquitous-economic-force/?source=app&frmapp=yes, accessed at 18:42, 8th August.

Kunthara, S. (2020) "What Happened To The Snacks? Some Companies Send Perks To Employees", available at https://news.crunchbase.com/news/what-happened-to-the-snacks-some-companies-send-perks-to-employees/, accessed at 18:23, 24th May.

McNamee, J. (2020) "The Online Events are here to Stay: Cookery Schools Go Online", *Irish Examiner*, December 6th, available at https://www.irishexaminer.com/lifestyle/food/arid-40129847.html, accessed at 17:52, 10th April.

Mitchell, 2019) "Think Hyperlocal: A Power Shift in Influencer Marketing", available at https://www.mitchcommgroup.com/2019/02/05/community-influencer-marketing/, accessed at 16:52, 4th October.

Nielsen Global Health and Wellness (2015) "We Are What We Eat: Healthy Eating Trends Around the World", available at https://www.scribd.com/document/283633003/Nielsen-Global-Health-and-Wellness-Report-We-Are-What-We-Eat-Healthy-Eating-Trends-Around-the-World-January-2015, accessed at 18:16, 10th July.

Powell, M. (2015) "Sneakernomics: Meet Gen Z", available at https://www.forbes.com/sites/mattpowell/2015/04/29/sneakernomics-meet-gen-z/?sh=56f2605f2c5c, accessed at 16:40, 1st October.

Quintiliani, L., Poulsen, S., and Sorensen, G. (2010) "Healthy Eating Strategies in the Workplace", International Journal of Workplace Health Management, available at https://www.emerald.com/insight/content/doi/10.1108/17538351011078929/full/html, accessed at 19:28, 11th Sept.

Reilly, C. (2017) "Who are Gen Z and what do they mean to market research", available at https://www.redcresearch.ie/who-are-gen-z/, accessed at 17:45, 27th July.

Short, E. (2019) "Why Food is Essential to Promoting Employee Wellness", available at https://www.siliconrepublic.com/advice/food-employee-wellness-health, accessed at 21:25, 24th March.

Singh, A. (2019) "Deliveroo Business Model | How Does Deliveroo Make Money?", available at https://www.feedough.com/deliveroo-business-model-how-does-deliveroo-make-money/, accessed at 22:15, 6th October.

Sodexco (2020) "Food 360: The New Workplace Food Landscape", available at https://www.sodexo.com/workreimagined/new-workplace-food-landscape.html, accessed at 18:45, 28th September.

The Happy Pear (2020) "The Happy Pear – Plant Based Cookery & Lifestyle", available at https://thehappypear.ie, accessed at 19:50, 19th March.

Yang, L. (2017) "13 Incredible perks of working at Google, according to Employees", available at https://www.insider.com, accessed at 17:05, 28th March.

Millennials in the Media

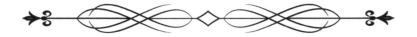

Meghann Scully, M.A.

Introduction

Millennials are those of us born in the 1980s until the early 2000s. I'm a Millennial as I was born in 1989, and I'm going to discuss my own experience working within the media industry.

Public speaking in school and a keen interest in communications led to a desire to work within the media industry. A few days during the 5th year spent in TG4 work shadowing further grew that interest.

Media studies it was to be. Perhaps lucky knowing my preferred college course during those teenage years but also no plan b in place. College syllabuses arrived into the school classrooms and corridors. The smell of a new book as pages were flipped open and we began the most important research of our lives.

I'd a particular yearning for Limerick and the University of Limerick. I had been on campus walking the grounds with my aunts, who had made Limerick home. As soon as I set foot on the lush green lawns with evergreens as far as the eye could see, I got a sense of 'I'm home'.

Plan A just became a whole lot more confined and restricted. Media in UL, and that was it. As I fanned those glossy pages, my heart was beating heavily against my chest. Did this book hold my destiny? At the age of 17, your college CAO/college application seems like the most important decision of your life. As I said. No plan B like many, if not most of my peers.

As mentioned earlier, I spent a few days in the TG4 studios in Connemara. I spent five years living in Spiddal during my national school days, and Gaeilge (Irish) was always my firm favourite subject. TG4 was the dream at that time. I watched those TG4 female presenters in awe. They were beautiful and always so stylish, presenting edgy shows such as Paisean Faisean, Eochair an Grá and the weather!

An Ghaeilge agus na Meáin Úra (Irish and New Media studies) right before my youthful eyes in the University of Limerick. Could this be real? My plan A course in my plan A University? The points were 370 as well, totally achievable, I felt for me. So I could apply for this course and not push myself too hard in the Leaving Cert. It seemed like a reasonable choice at the time.

I could enjoy my final year in secondary school, take time with friends, spend weekends socialising and riding ponies while also playing camogie. I saw my peers stressed, worried, having sleepless nights as they spent every hour of every day studying.

The Leaving Cert exams came and went, and a summer of fun and activities followed. Music festivals, horse shows and time outdoors. While at Millstreet Horse show in August of that summer, I befriended fellow Galwegians in the club. We were all leaving certs and had gotten our results, and now we waited for the CAO/ college offers. One of the girls had also applied for the same course as I in UL. Two weeks later, I walked into my very first Irish lecture, and as I opened the door, a familiar face waved my way, and so began An Ghaeilge Agus na Meáin Úra and the next four years of my life. I'll be honest. I had more interest in the college lifestyle than the college studies. Saying that, in four years, I managed to never once fail an exam as I was a crammer and always did just enough.

It was the semester in Malta during third year that it all became real. Six months in a sunny climate and learning journalism from the night-time editor of The Times Of Malta. I came back from Malta with more freckles and a more profound interest in media and journalism. I approached An Focal, the University newspaper, and so began my first column and the student papers first beauty column. A Masters in Journalism became my new goal in NUI Galway.

UL came and went before my eyes, but an acceptance into the Masters course in Galway took me on another adventure. During that year, I did work experience in Galway Bay FM, wrote some articles for the Galway Advertiser and had a radio show on the college radio station, Flirt FM. My blog also began that year, an online CV of my published work to flash before employers post-Graduation.

2012 was a bleak time as a Millennial fresh from University. Jobs were few and far between. Unpaid Internship seemed to be the buzz term. Unpaid, working for free and minimal pay became the norm for five years.

I landed an internship with MTV in London in 2013, and it was paid. It seemed too good to be true. I landed over in April of that year. I was enthusiastic, eager, spritely and energetic. I was ready to take this year on and learn and earn as much knowledge about broadcast media. The thought of working alongside such talented people felt exhilarating.

The year was very much that way, but I felt this Millennial was pulled down a few pegs and made aware that my dreams of being a presenter were unattainable. One colleague told me I was "too friendly" as I spoke to everyone in the office. The same colleague told me I should work in production/ behind the scenes. I felt deflated. I spent the year studying the presenters and different styles and used the time to pick up some tips. When I was shooting red carpet events, I always shot a piece to camera (presenter talking down the lens) for my practice, but it was later questioned by another colleague. Fellow Millennials who were slightly older. It took me a few years to realise that this industry was cut-throat, and many people would try to take me down, steer me off course and manipulate and coerce me.

It was an eye-opening experience. I returned to Ireland in 2014 and decided to walk away from media and five years of studies. I entered the world of PR and got a paid job almost instantly. Six months later, I walked away. I couldn't deal with one more excel sheet. Sitting in front of a computer all day drained my creative soul. So here I was unemployed, told I couldn't make it in the media, but I knew I couldn't spend another day in a Monday- Friday, 9-5 role.

There began another year of unpaid work in media, hoping one day it might fall into place and someone might offer me a paid role. After a year and a half in Dublin, I moved home to Galway, broke and broken. My family begged me to become a teacher, so I applied for the HDip. I knew deep down I didn't want to be a teacher, but I couldn't go on being an unpaid journalist. Every time I applied for a role, I got offered an unpaid internship. It was simply soul-destroying. Employers admired my glistening CV and multimedia experience but used the recession as a buzzword. As though I should feel honoured to have even been offered an unpaid position in their company. But I kept going because no matter how many times I fell, I kept getting back up.

Since 2016 I have been working in the media and getting paid. By the time I was 30, I had thought I would have my own house, be on great money, and not think about my next paycheck. I often look at current job roles and notice that Gen Z are setting up companies, internships, more often than not, are paid, or grad programmes are there for every area of employment. When I was a college student, the only grad programmes that existed were corporate orientated.

I even notice with Gen Z how advanced they are when it comes to social media apps, having the latest technology, and seeing the tech generation. They are savvy, ever-changing and ahead of the trend. TikTok is one example of how Gen Z are dominating that app. 18-year-olds are making incredible money from these quick, snappy videos.

In the last few years, the word influencer has become synonymous with social media. People with huge followings influencing the audience on what products they should buy.

Many of these products are paid for promotions, and more and more companies are using these people for marketing campaigns over traditional media. Influencers are earning from their own Instagram profiles. It's now a career and something many school goers strive to do and want to become.

It comes with its downside. These people have become social media celebrities in some senses, exposing their every move to the masses. Lines become blurred, and 'followers' want to know more and feel entitled to getting this information. There has also been the issue of editing photos, changing body shapes using editing tools and false advertising to young, impressionable people. Trolling has become far too common, people sending nasty messages to these influencers, usually from fake profiles, with no profile picture.

I use my social media platforms to showcase my work within the media. In recent years, I have obtained some paid promotional work or collaborations with brands when they give me products to try for free to promote on my account. I've passed 10,000 followers on Instagram, which is seen as the golden number because it means I can now add a 'swipe up' link on my Instagram stories, I can direct followers straight to a brands website which is what they want, hits on their website, traffic and hopefully sales. The term used for those of us with over 10k followers is microblogger/ influencer. Brands might choose to work with a handful of microbloggers or else one larger blogger depending on who they want to target.

I consider myself a broadcaster and author and not an influencer per se, but due to my following, I fall under that micro tab as well. Being able to earn from social media has been an added bonus, especially during the uncertain year that was the pandemic, as revenue fell from MC and public speaking engagements as they were all cancelled.

As for connectedness, social media allowed me to stay connected with friends and family during the pandemic, as many are online. But it also made me dependent on my phone almost all the time. I have set boundaries on my social media use. I will interact with followers, but I will always put family and friends first and give them the majority of my time online. This is very important because we can sometimes feel that we must converse with people we don't even know, and before we know it, we have spent hours on our phones. I often felt guilted into replying to every single person that messaged me. Still, on many occasions, it became uncomfortable whereby the person would become inappropriate or start demanding more information about me, so I had to take a step back and stop sharing so much about my personal life significantly as my followers grew. I've seen what larger influencers have had to endure from trolls, which has added to my personal boundaries online. If I share less, I'll have less chance of trolling.

While it is nice to chat with people online, we have to disconnect from those we do not know online and reconnect with those in our homes. Phoneless time is critical. My phone is set on 'sleep mode', whereby it knocks off at a specific time, meaning it won't ring or buzz throughout the night and disturb my sleep. When I am in company, I will often set my phone to Airplane Mode and leave it in my bag to make the most of real life, human interaction.

I now have to view my social media as part of my working day, setting hours to go online and be offline. In the years post graduating, knowing my worth has become a phrase I've had to really drill into my head. Now, when asked to give my services, I weigh it up. I've learned to say 'no' or send over my fee because I can't do everything for free. I am a professional, my work is valuable, and like everyone else, our time is precious.

On Being an 'Influencer'
Is this the New Dream Career Option for Younger Generations?

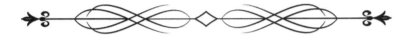

Darina Callanan, MA.

Influencing as a Marketing Tool

Over recent years, what are known as 'influencers' have increasingly used their social media platforms as marketing tools. Influencers strive to build effective and trustworthy relationships with their followers; therefore, it comes as no surprise why companies send influencers different items to advertise on their social media platforms.

In 2021, COVID-19 had a devasting impact on businesses all over the world which has led to the question, are influencers struggling in this current pandemic or are they excelling? Has it got even worse in 2021? Taylor (2020) states that this has not been the case for influencers as they normally prepare and record their content from home, and they might have slightly adjusted their content to be applicable for the pandemic. Taylor (2020) further adds that influencers on Instagram had an average increase in likes of 67.7% and over a 50% increase in comments. Arguably, in a report by Love UX, reduced marketing budgets due to Covid-19, has had a knock-on effect for influencers. In the report, over 500 Instagram influencers were analysed, and the results showed that 65% of the influencers posted less sponsored adds during the pandemic resulting in a loss of income.

Although it is evident that influencer marketing is effective for many companies, there still lies the question of ethical credibility of the influencer and the product they are trying to promote. Due to the relationships that influencers build with their followers, it is up to the followers to make the decision whether they believe in the products the influencer is selling or not!

There are many statistics on the internet confirming the effectiveness of influencer marketing and according to Baker (2020) 80% of marketers agree that it is an effective way of marketing over other marketing channels. Nowadays, influencers can be seen all over our social media apps. It is evident that becoming an influencer is a popular career option for Generation Z and maybe this is because they are the first generation to grow up with full access to technology and a host of media platforms. When we are flicking through our social media, we all see the glitz and the glam of being an influencer; whether it is the clothes, makeup, holidays or just lifestyle in general! But is it as glamourous as we think? In this chapter, we sift through all things 'influencer' and we also interviewed two influencers to get a better insight into their social media lives and personas.

Influencing: What is it?

An influencer is a term used to describe an individual who can have an influence over people's thinking and behaviour on social media platforms. There are many different types of social media influencers such as YouTubers and bloggers who, not only use the platform to share their thoughts and ideas to their followers, but to also make money from marketing companies to promote certain products or travel destinations. Today, there are online job descriptions and job opportunities that people can apply for to become an influencer! Although influencers have taken over the majority of our social media feeds, there is still an 'unknown' about their roles and the perceptions that both the older and younger generations have towards influencers.

Influencing as a Career Option

There have been many different opinions over the years about whether influencing is a 'real' full time job. The career option as an 'influencer' has definite ties with social media and technology which have allowed both Millennials and Generation Z to explore this new avenue of work. Influencers use their social media platforms to create 'followers' and the more followers they have…the more money they potentially make!

A few years ago, you might have asked a child what they wanted to be when they grew up and you would get typical answers like, 'I want to be a firefighter', 'I want to be a teacher' or 'I want to be a doctor'. However, if you ask a child now what they would like to be when they grow up, 'an influencer' is definitely a career option they might well say. In a recent study by Awin, it was proven that 'social media influencer' stood second at 17 percent and third at 14 percent, as the most popular professions children wish to pursue as a career (Malik, 2019).

An influencer's social media account is driven by a specific kind of identity production which is based on what the influencer posts, shares and likes. Their social media pages are often edited snapshots of how they want to be seen by their followers (Khamis, Ang and Welling, 2016). Social media has provided a platform which accommodates ordinary people to share their stories with other users, but also to follow the lifestyles of the rich and famous. In this current climate, the social media platforms provide the opportunity for 'ordinary people' to turn into 'celebrities' if they reach a certain number of followers. Millennials, Generation Z and the younger generations are seeing these 'ordinary people' turn somewhat 'famous' and are, increasingly, attracted to that lifestyle hence choosing influencing as a career option.

How do Influencers Earn Money and How Much do Influencers Earn?

It may come as a surprise to many, but those global influencers at the top of their game can earn millions through advertisements and building their own businesses through their social media platforms. Influencers create engaging and unique content for their followers which may involve advertising clothing brands, makeup lines or a collaboration they may be involved in with other companies. If the content they post is good enough, they are more than likely going to create satisfying revenue for themselves.

The top ten influencers in Ireland for 2020 consisted of 3

Generation Z and 7 Millennials with two Generation Z hogging the first two places. The top ten influencers vary in what they promote and their content but one thing they all have in common is that they use their social media accounts, in particular, Instagram, to engage with their followers. The top Irish influencer in Ireland Nicole O'Brien earns between €2,202- €3671 per Instagram post and last year she earned an astonishing €422,992 (Langford, 2021). As well as earning hundreds of thousands, people use social media to create and promote their business. A beauty influencer, Aimee Connolly, created her own business 'Sculpted by Aimee' and with over 79k followers on Instagram she promotes and advertises new and current products. Aimee Connolly started her business at 23 years of age and now at 28, she is earning €5.4 million in sales despite the disruption of COVID-19 (Independent, 2021).

It is evident from the recent findings of 2020 that Generation Z are making their way to the top when it comes to Influencing. Millennials you better watch out and make room for the Gen Zers!

What does it take to be an Influencer?

When you ask influencers how they came to be an influencer, some might say, 'It just happened' or some influencers might say they wanted to make a career from the social media platforms and share their thoughts and ideas on what they love such as the gym, makeup and many more!

There are numerous online articles and blogs on how to become an influencer and even step by step guides! A few years ago, it might have seemed impossible to become an influencer if you were not already a celebrity, but in today's world you can find out tips and tricks in becoming a successful influencer. As the world evolves, more individuals have opinions on certain topics.

Being an influencer in 2021 is not as straight forward as it seems. You not only have to be consistent and present on social media platforms by posting pictures or posting videos, you also need to be conscious of individuals' opinions and if people are going to agree with you or write negative comments. And, keyboard warriors are not shy in this regard.

One question to keep in mind, is it all as glamourous as it seems? I have interviewed two Irish Generation Z influencers, one influencer who is in the beauty and fashion industry and an upcoming influencer who is in the beauty industry, that are dominating the current social media platforms to find out more.

Interview one: Robyn McManus

(Robyn currently has 10.7k followers on Instagram and her content is based on makeup, fashion and sharing positivity)

Section 1

DC: Are you a Millenial or a Generation Z?

RM: Generation Z.

DC: What is your understanding of the term 'Influencer'?

RM: Well, I suppose it has a lot of different meanings, a lot of people would say it is different things. But I would say I think it can be seen negatively and it is probably the wrong term to use. There are some people who are influencing things that they receive so I think they would be a promoter rather than an influencer. Then on the other side, you have influencers who are sharing their thoughts and ideas so there is so many different meanings to the word. I would have never called myself an influencer before until you contacted me! But when I talked to people, they said that I kind of am so I suppose am I!

DC: Do you think social media platforms are essential to becoming an influencer? If yes, why?

RM: Yes, absolutely. That is what it is all based on and social media marketing. I mean I would not use any other platform other than Instagram to do my influencing. I don't have any other social media platforms; I mean I have a Facebook account but I haven't gone on that in years.

DC: Do you think influencing would be possible without social media?

RM: No way. I don't think the term would be associated with anything else. I mean there is no other way to influence really.

DC: How Important/unimportant do you see influencers in today's society?

RM: I suppose it depends on the generation. It is really important for some age groups. When Covid- 19 happened and when the restrictions were lifted a little bit, I wasn't looking at the news to tell me what I could do. I was logging on to Instagram and seeing what other people were doing. I think it can be very important especially during the pandemic.

DC: How did you become an influencer?

RM: For me, I did makeup years ago before social media was a big thing and I used to do weddings, TV and then I completely stopped. Last summer, I decided I wanted to get back into it. So, what I did was reach out to loads of influencers and told them that I would do their makeup for different events so I could get more exposure. When I was doing their makeup, I realised I wanted to do the same thing as them and I didn't want to be that person who was giving the perks to other people, I wanted to get perks too. I started to become friends with the influencers and I just realised that I wanted to do the same thing!

Section 2:

DC: Who is your main audience - Millennials or Generation Z or mixture of both?

RM: It is a mixture of both definitely. My following would be mostly female, 85% of my following would be female. It is a lot of women of all different ages that I would chat with.

DC: Do you think influencing is a potential career path?

RM: I personally don't. I believe it can become a career if you go on a reality tv show and get a large following and you get noticed. But I have seen a lot of girls who have burned out already that are my age and who have reached their peak. I have recognised that it is a long-term thing, not a short-term thing and it is important to recognise that. I think the content you share is important and I have no problem going on social media and talking about my mental health because a lot of people can relate.

DC: Who do you think is more successful in the current climate - Millenial or Generation Z influencers?

RM: I think the Millennials are more successful on social media, but I don't know if that is because they are more aware. I don't know many people that are younger that are doing influencing.

DC: What do you think is the most important thing about being an influencer?

RM: The most important thing for me is to be real and to be yourself but some people do get far for not being themselves, so it is hard to say. I really don't know. Personally, I have progressed on my social media platform because I have talked about normal things and I don't pretend to be someone that I am not.

DC: Did you find it difficult to attract your current audience?

RM: No, I don't really know to be honest! In the early days when I was doing makeup I would constantly go on social media and follow people and they would follow me back to get my followers up but that was a while ago. Now, people share things that I put up so yeah it is just hard to say.

DC: If you could change one thing (if any) what would you change about the influencer community?

RM: Like what I said at the start, I would not have considered myself an influencer because there is so many different meanings to the word. There can be people who are different on social media to what they are in real life, like on Facebook years ago, there was no filters or taking hours to take a photo, it was more real life. People who are influencing are at the top of the food chain on social media and if you're not being real then it's not fair on the people who follow you. I know you touch base on mental health in the next section, but sometimes Instagram might not be the best place if you are not in the right headspace. Sometimes it is just not reality and sometimes it's hard to know what is real and what is not.

Section 3

DC: Do you think influencing can have an effect on mental health?

RM: Yes, it does one hundred percent. I would have to say that it does not always have a negative impact because I think it can have a positive impact too talking from my own experience. If I am having a bad day and share it on Instagram, I come on to get it out and talk about it. I live with my friend and sometimes I wouldn't go into her and talk about it because it would feel a bit much. But looking at a screen and talking about it made me more comfortable and I felt that I could, and it really helped me. But not only that, when people start to reply to you and saying lovely things and sharing their stories, it really boosts you up. Everyone goes through stuff and there is a real side to Instagram, but it has that side which is negative because you are in competition with so many people and it can be really tough on your head. For me personally, I think it is more positive than negative because it has been a real safe place for me, and I have been so lucky with my following because they are so interactive and kind. I have made friends with people who I might not ever meet but it's my little family and happy place.

Interview Two: Charleen Murphy

(Charleen currently has 91.1k followers on Instagram and her content is based on Fashion and positivity)

Section 1

DC: Are you a Millenial or a Generation Z?

CM: Generation Z.

DC: What is your understanding of the term 'Influencer'?

CM: I feel an influencer is someone who has power over what people buy or influencing someone on what to buy. I don't feel like you need to have a massive following to be an influencer. I know girls that don't have that many followers, but people trust their opinion. So, I think an influencer is someone who can be trusted.

DC: Do you think social media platforms are essential to becoming an influencer? If yes, why?

CM: Yes, I think so because if there wasn't social media platforms, it would be word of mouth and that can only go so far with people. But with the social media platforms you can reach all over the world if you want to, so I do think social media is essential to become an influencer.

DC: Do you think influencing would be possible without social media?

CM: No, I don't think so. I think that social media is steering away from TV and radio and I feel that social media is needed for influencing.

DC: How Important/unimportant do you see influencers in today's society?

CM: I think it is a bit of both. A lot of time people think that influencers are air heads or walking advertisements, but I do think people see the importance in influencers too. Especially with the Black Lives Matter movement people were looking to influencers for information. I think is important for influencers to share important messages and if you have a big following it is important to do the right thing, so I do think that we are important in today's society.

DC: How did you become an influencer?

CM: An influencer came into my school when I was sixteen and gave a talk on blogging and things like that and I was really interested because I love fashion and makeup. I then started my own blog on a website, but I didn't really tell anyone so if you aren't sharing it how are people going to know about it. I kind of stopped that then and started to post on Instagram more and started to use more hashtags and posting pictures. I started to share some things that I bought and doing hauls and I think when you start being consistent that when it your following starts getting bigger.

Section 2

DC: Who is your main audience - Millennials or Generation Z or mixture of both?

CM: My main audience would be 18-24 so it would be Generation Z.

DC: Do you think influencing is a potential career path?

CM: Definitely, I have seen people do it in the past and now. But what worries me and why I am still in college, is that Instagram and other social media platforms could just shut down and that is what freaks me out. Especially during coronavirus, I was talking to a few girls who do it full time and they said that a few of their brand deals were getting pulled because people do not have the money to pay influencers. That is what really shook me so I do think it is good to have as a career path but I think having something you can do as well on the side is a good idea because you just never know.

DC: Who do you think is more successful in the current climate - Millenial or Generation Z influencers?

CM: I am not sure. I think Millennials would be making more money from it because they would have started earlier than Generation Z so they would have a bigger following. I feel that some of the brands Millennials work with would be bigger so they would have a bigger budget to work with. But I do think the up and coming influencers might be more trusted in away. The bigger you get on the social media platforms the more hate you are going to get. But in terms of money, I think the Millennials are more successful but I do think Generation Z will be more successful when we are that age.

DC: What do you think is the most important thing about being an influencer?

CM: I think staying true to yourself a being honest about stuff. I would not go on social media and bash something because that is just not me and I am not that type of person. I wouldn't go on social media platforms and say I love something if I don't, I just won't talk about it. I just think being authentic and honest is important and you do have a responsibility to be a good influencer.

DC: Did you find it difficult to attract your current audience?

CM: No not really especially now on Instagram the algorithm is kind of difficult. When I first start out, I don't know where all of the followers came from it was just so much quicker I think. But now I feel like you need to put in a lot more work to get the followers especially when you are a bit bigger. I am on 50k followers now and a lot of people probably already know you from Ireland so if they like you, they are probably would. So, I don't find it too hard.

DC: If you could change one thing (if any) what would you change about the influencer community?

CM: Probably just people who are doing it to get free stuff because I feel like a lot of people have started blogging now. I think if there are too many a lot of people might be looking for free stuff and it might make other influencers less trustworthy nearly. If it is an overly saturated market, it might make it become less good of a market. So, I think just people who are in it for the right reasons but everyone is really lovely and I wouldn't change anything about the people.

Section 3

DC: Do you think influencing can have an effect on mental health?

CM: Maybe a little bit. There are definitely times when you have pressure to post and you always have to be switched on so it can be a bit draining sometimes. But if I feel that I am getting like that or anxious I will just slow down myself and not post as much. I do think there is more pros than cons to it, but I think having a bit of anxiety and pressure comes with it when you have a large following. I do think there are more good things than bad things.

The above two snapshot interviews illustrate that there are onerous responsibilities associated with being an influencer in terms of creating a safe and relatable platform for their followers.

References and Suggested Reading

Baker, K. (2020). *What Will Influencer Marketing Look Like In 2020?.* [online] Blog.hubspot.com. Available at: <https://blog.hubspot.com/marketing/how-to-work-with-influencers> [Accessed 17 August 2020].

Coogan, K. and Crowley- Henry, M., 2020. *Meet Your New Workmates: Generation Z's Views On Work And Careers.* [online] RTE.ie. Available at: <https://www.rte.ie/brainstorm/2019/1003/1080884-meet-your-new-workmates-generation-zs-views-on-work-and-careers/> [Accessed 11 June 2020].

Gomez, K., Mawhinney, T. and Betts, K. ed., 2019. *Welcome To Generation Z.* Deloitte, pp.1-24.

Independent, (2021). Beauty influencer's brand posts €5.4m sales amid Covid comfort shopping. [online] Available at: <https://www.independent.ie/business/irish/beauty-influencers-brand-posts-54m-sales-amid-covid-comfort-shopping-39972137.html> [Accessed 5 March 2021].

Khamis, S., Ang, L. and Welling, R. (2016). Self-branding, 'micro-celebrity' and the rise of Social Media Influencers. *Celebrity Studies*, 8(2), pp.191-208.

Langford, R. (2021). Revealed: The Top 10 Irish Influencers - Netimperative. [online] Netimperative. Available at: <https://www.netimperative.com/2020/11/27/revealed-the-top-10-irish-influencers/> [Accessed 5 March 2021].

Malik, D., 2019. *Research Proves 'Influencer' As One Of The Most Popular Career Options Among Children.* [online] Digitalinformationworld.com. Available at: <https://www.digitalinformationworld.com/2019/02/young-affiliates-children-aspire-to-be-social-media-influencers-youtubers.html> [Accessed 12 May 2020].

Nevitte, C. 2019. *What Generation Z Want From Their Employee*

Experience. [online] People Management. Available at: <https://www.peoplemanagement.co.uk/voices/comment/what-generation-z-want-from-employee-experience> [Accessed 11 June 2020].

Seabridge, M. (2020). *The Impact Of Coronavirus On Instagram Influencers — Love UX*. [online] Love UX. Available at: <https://loveux.co.uk/insights/the-impact-of-coronavirus-on-instagram-influencers> [Accessed 18 August 2020].

Sladek, S. and Grabinger, A. (2014). Gen Z: The first generation of the 21st Century has arrived!. [online] Xyzuniversity.com. Available at: https://www.xyzuniversity.com/wp-content/uploads/2018/08/GenZ_Final-dl1.pdf [Accessed 11 June 2020].

Taylor, C. (2020). *Is COVID Making Marketing Influencers More Influential?*. [online] Forbes. Available at: <https://www.forbes.com/sites/charlesrtaylor/2020/07/30/is-covid-making-marketing-influencers-more-influential/#55a513aa4200> [Accessed 17 August 2020].

The Dynamic Duo Authors

Darina Callanan is a HR Professional who started her career at 22 years old. She is passionate about all things Human Resources and has a particular interest when it comes to multigenerational workforces, employee engagement and the new trends that are faced by HR. Darina both studied and works in Human Resources and is fascinated on how the workforce changes on a day-to-day basis! You can learn more about Darina via her social media platforms – Instagram and LinkedIn.

Susan McKenna has worked in direct practice and in management in social care environments in the south east of Ireland, the mid-west and the west. She was an Erasmus scholar in Europe and has written and published widely on a range of themes in mental health and wellness both in Ireland and abroad. She is Director of Book Hub Publishing and reps a range of authors.

You can learn more about Susan on www.bookhubpublishing.com and via her social media platforms – Instagram and LinkedIn.

Contributing Author Biographies

Catherine Fitzgibbon (aka The Culinary Celt) is a media sales and marketing professional for the past 22 years. She is passionate about exploring contemporary culinary experiences and actively promotes the areas of food sustainably and food tourism through her food blogs, writing contributions and other marketing activities, using an ethically-based farm to fork ethos. Catherine is also a consultant in the areas of Food Tourism & Millennial Culture with the Dissertation Doctors Clinic.

You can learn more about Catherine on www.theculinarycelt.com and via her social media platforms – @theculinarycelt

Instagram, Twitter, Facebook, Pinterest, and YouTube.

Jennifer Murphy has worked for the past thirteen years in various Human Resource roles in Retail, Manufacturing and, most recently, the Hospitality sector. She is a highly strategic HR professional and is passionate about Culture and Talent Management. Jennifer has had the honour of working in some of the most prestigious business locations in Ireland and, to date, has looked after ten such properties.

More recently, she consults with the DocCheck.Com in the area of HR and research perspectives.

You can learn more about Jennifer on her LinkedIn profile.

Dr Phil Noone is a Mindfulness Teacher/Practitioner who has lectured in the School of Nursing and Midwifery at NUIGalway for the past 17 years. She is passionate about health and well-being, holds an MA in Health Promotion and an MSc in Mindfulness Based Interventions.

Her research interests and published work include health topics such as stress, suicide, habit formation, happiness, student well-being and Mindfulness. Phil has a deep love and connection to nature and is currently exploring the power of open water sea-swimming in conjunction with Dr Niall MacGiolla Bhuí from TheDocCheck.com and Cliona Beirne, due for publication in Mental Health For Millennials Volume 5 in October 2021. She is also completing a book on 'Home', due to be published later in 2021.

You can learn more about Dr Noone via her social media platforms – on Instagram and Facebook.

Meghann Scully is a broadcaster and author. She has written two books, 'Broken Love' and 'Little Pocket of Love' and contributed a chapter to each Mental Health for Millennials book in our Book Hub Publishing series. She is from Galway and is a sports fan as well as keeping active herself with a keen interest in travel.

Meghann is a regular contributor on social media and mainstream media speaking on themes of loss and grief in addition to acting as MC on a range of social events in a national context.

You can learn more about Meghann via her social media platforms –Instagram, Twitter, Facebook and LinkedIn.

About The Editor

Dr. Niall MacGiolla Bhuí holds a doctorate in psychology and was, for several years, a senior lecturer in Humanities. A founding editor and editor-in-chief of the Irish Journal of Applied Studies for a decade, he is a senior editor with three decades experience in publishing and has had several of his own books published in Ireland, Canada and the United States in addition to co-authoring books and journal papers with colleagues. He is, along with Dr. Phil Noone, series editor of the Mental Health For Millennials seven volume series (2017-2023). Niall is currently writing about the psychology of open water sea swimming in the context of resilience.